Visual Explorer®
Revised and Expanded

Facilitator's Guide

Charles J. Palus and David Magellan Horth
Center for Creative Leadership

CCL Stock No. 00755D

ISBN 978-1-60491-864-9

©2014 Center for Creative Leadership

Published by Center for Creative Leadership

Sylvester Taylor, Director of Assessments, Tools, and Publications

Peter Scisco, Manager, Publication Development

Kelly Lombardino, Manager, Publication Dissemination

Karen Lewis, Associate Editor

Contributors: Robert Burnside, Cheryl De Ciantis, Bill Drath, Bruce Flye, Steadman Harrison III, Greg Laskow, The Leading Creatively Airlie Community, Kelly Lombardino, Mary Lynn Pulley, TZiPi Radonsky, Lyndon Rego, Chris and Signe Schaefer, Peter Scisco, Al Selvin, Hamish Taylor, Martin Wilcox, and so many more.

Layout: Joanne Ferguson

Visual Explorer Quick Guide

Group dialogue can be difficult for any number of reasons, such as hidden conflict, power differentials among group members, an unclear idea of the problem the group faces, and group or organizational norms that make some topics off limits. Visual Explorer is grounded in years of research and practice that shows the power of images and objects to enable effective dialogues about complex issues. There are five basic steps to using Visual Explorer as a way to facilitate a group conversation. Turn this page over for a walkthrough of those basic steps. You can alter or elaborate on these steps for particular situations.

What Is Visual Explorer?

Visual Explorer uses images to facilitate conversations, creating new perspectives and shared understanding. The tool consists of 216 images, available in letter-size (USA), postcard-size, and playing-card-size formats, and a facilitator's guide.

Visual Explorer Benefits

Visual Explorer offers the most benefits when a group has objectives such as

- seeking patterns in complex issues and making connections
- seeking a variety of perspectives
- asking new questions
- eliciting stories and creating metaphors
- tapping into personal experiences and passions
- articulating what is known to the group
- creating or practicing dialogue
- building on ideas
- surfacing and channeling emotions and intuitions
- exploring the landscape of a complex set of issues
- imagining alternatives
- sparking humor and playfulness

1 FRAME

Choose one or two focal questions to frame the conversation. For example, a group facing a shared challenge might ask

- What is the key to this challenge we are facing?
- What strengths do we have for solving this challenge?

2 BROWSE

Make the VE images available for browsing. Everyone in the group should silently browse the images, and each person should choose an image for each framing question. The connection between image and question can be literal, or it may be emotional, metaphorical, aesthetic, or intuitive.

5 EXTEND

After this initial dialogue, a certain kind of momentum is often present in the group. It can extend its conversation in whatever direction it thinks is important. Subsequently, the most significant images and metaphors can be reused in ongoing creative problem solving, invention, and communication. The images from the group often lend themselves to cascading to other groups in the organization, broadening the conversation and the creative thinking.

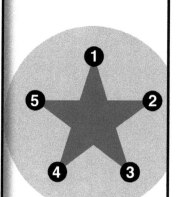

3 REFLECT

Each person examines the image he or she has selected, and reflects on how the image connects to the framing question. During reflection, encourage the people in the group to pay close attention to the image they have selected and ask themselves

- What is the image?
- What is happening in it?
- What is the context of the picture?
- Is there anything surprising in the image?
- How does the picture connect to the framing questions?

4 SHARE

The group convenes and sits in a circle. One person at a time shares his or her image(s), following a four-part pattern.

1. Each person shows a picture and describes the image itself. At this point, the individual does not talk about connecting the picture to the framing question. Instead, he or she talks about what the picture is, what is happening in the picture, and details that she or he notices in the picture.
2. The person describes the connection he or she has made between the image and the framing question and can explain how the image is a response to the question.
3. Each person in the group responds to the image(s) offered by the speaker, following the same pattern. First, the response focuses on what is in the picture, whether the responder sees the same things that other members of the group or the first speaker sees, and what details stand out.
4. Second, the responder describes the connections he or she can make between the image and the framing question.
5. After each speaker has shared an image in this way, he or she thanks the group, and the conversation moves on to the next person and image(s). The conversation continues until everyone has shared the chosen images.

Contents

Introduction

Visual Explorer is a set of images and methods for supporting collaborative, creative conversations in a wide variety of situations. The images are deliberately diverse and global in subject, context, and aesthetics, and range from food to space travel, from birth to death, from organization to complexity and chaos. The images invite examination—they are visually interesting. The images invite connections—they provide metaphors and help carry ideas and insights.

Visual Explorer is grounded in research and practice that shows the power of images and objects to enable effective dialogues about complex issues (Burnside & Guthrie, 1992; De Ciantis, 1995; Edwards, 1987; Geschka, 1990; Morgan, 1997; Palus & Horth, 2002; Young & Dixon, 1996). A widely known tool often referred to as "the postcard exercise" was the initial prototype for Visual Explorer (Palus & Drath, 2001; Rosinski, 2003; Schaefer, 1993).

What Is Visual Explorer?

Visual Explorer creates dialogue and produces insights by combining images with one or more framing questions. As a tool for leadership and leadership development, Visual Explorer helps people build shared direction, alignment, and commitment amid multiple perspectives (for more on the idea of direction, alignment, and commitment, see Drath et al., 2008).

Visual Explorer is not a team exercise, game, or simulation in the sense that most facilitators, human resource professionals, and training-program participants understand those experiences. There is no single right way to use it. Many facilitators use it to assist people with important or difficult conversations. Dialogue in groups can be difficult for any number of reasons, such as hidden conflict, power differentials among group members, an unclear idea of the problem the group faces, the inability to envision a solution, and group or organizational norms that

EXPLORING ACROSS CULTURES

Tom Boydell, director of Inter-Logics and a coauthor of a book about organizational learning (see Pedlar, Burgoyne, and Boydell, 1998), recently wrote to us about his use of Visual Explorer.

> We use Visual Explorer for exploring almost any concept—not just leadership. We also use it quite often in action-learning settings, when we ask people to describe where they have got to in their ongoing projects. As things have worked out, we have used it more outside of the United Kingdom, especially in Jordan, Syria, and Egypt. In the latter, we used it many times on a large project with the Egyptian Post Office. We have also used it several times on a program for a Danish multinational— fifteen different nationalities including North and South America, Europe, Asia, and Africa were rep- resented on each occasion. From all I've said here, I think you can gather that we have found it to work really well in a wide variety of cultures.

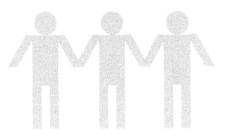

make some topics off limits. Visual Explorer adapts well to all of those situations and many others—including personal reflection in which the dialogue is an internal one.

Visual Explorer does not necessarily require a trained facilitator to achieve its results. A team leader or member can, with the benefit of this facilitator's guide and a little practice, guide groups through a Visual Explorer session to remarkable outcomes. Visual Explorer is somewhat self-correcting and forgiving, such that the default process tends to be a positive one—a good conversation supported by meaningful imagery. Of course, situations that involve difficult problems will benefit from a facilitator with prior experience and advanced group-work skills.

What Does Visual Explorer Do?

The objective for groups using Visual Explorer is to enable their members to collectively explore a complex topic from a variety of perspectives. Visual Explorer can play a role in a larger process of addressing business challenges, but alone it doesn't create decisions or actions. Instead, it helps groups understand the context and the perspectives that surround the decisions they make.

Using Visual Explorer

One of Visual Explorer's greatest strengths is its versatility. Although its original applications focused on groups of managers and leaders in organizational settings, it has been used effectively in a wide variety of settings—for example, in education (preschool through adult), in marketing focus groups, and in one-on-one coaching. This facilitator's guide describes a number of those alternative methods and applications. Over the years Visual Explorer has been in use, facilitators and users have found it helpful in situations and applications such as

- seeking patterns in complex issues and making connections

- surfacing a variety of perspectives

- provoking new questions

- eliciting stories and creating metaphors

- tapping into personal experiences and passions

- articulating what has been unspoken or "undiscussable"

- constructively relating with others through dialogue

How Does Visual Explorer Work?

Think of Visual Explorer as enabling a *third language* among people. Why would you need a third language? Consider how each of us has a personal world of meaning and expression that differs from that of others. If we share a common language—English or Spanish, for example—we can use that as common ground to build agreement, especially if we're talking about simple things (for example, "that blue car over there is mine"). But as the ideas become more complex, it becomes harder to get across our intent to another person, and we can't rely only on the common ground of a shared vocabulary. There is a better chance that we will misinterpret the other person or simply not understand what he or she is trying to get us to see. This challenge is exacerbated when group

BRIDGING LANGUAGE DIFFERENCES

Our colleague Jeff Yip studies the practice of crossing social boundaries in organizations (see Ernst and Yip, 2009). He tells a story about using Visual Explorer at a conference in which participants spoke many different languages:

> I used Visual Explorer in a workshop with young journalists from ten countries in Southeast Asia: Vietnam, Cambodia, Laos, Myanmar, Singapore, Malaysia, Brunei, Philippines, Thailand, and Indonesia. These young people represent a region grouping known as ASEAN (Association of Southeast Asian Nations). Many of them have lived through experiences of conflict and poverty. The participants all spoke different languages; English was not their first language. By using Visual Explorer as a third language, they were able to share with each other their deep fears and their aspirations for the region.
>
> During this session, each person composed a framing question as a way of sharing their diverse perspectives on the issues of the region. The response from a young woman from Vietnam was particularly moving (see Figure 1): "How can ASEAN governments stop human trafficking across the boundaries, especially women and children? There are Indonesian women who are made prostitutes or Vietnamese women who are displayed in a market for men to choose and buy. The image I picked is a bowl of multicolored fruit-flavored cereal deep in milk. Some of the cereal pieces are floating; some are down in the milk; some try to be afloat by sitting on another one. From a normal, positive point of view, this photo is full of colors and looks delicious. But it appears to me that women and children are very precious, yet they are in some areas of ASEAN countries suffering from being placed in dark situations and seem not to have control over their own lives. They are asking for help. We need to discover the core causes of the problem before solving it. Here in the picture, we can see all the different pieces in the bowl of milk. If we take out the milk, all of them may be saved! And yet, there are some people who like the milk, so we need to compromise."

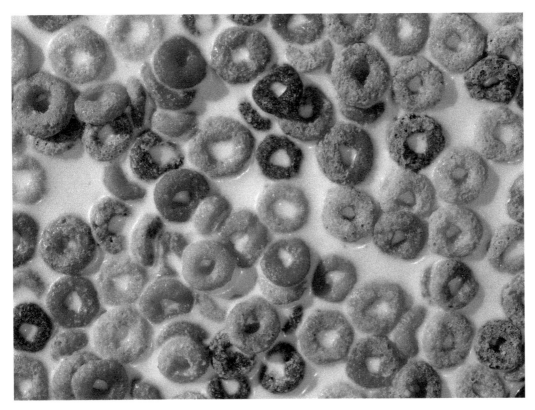

Figure 1. For one Visual Explorer participant, multiple colors suggests the complexity of dealing with human trafficking. *Photographs provided by Getty Images, Inc., ©2004. All Rights Reserved.*

members speak different languages, as they might if they are working across geographical boundaries.

Visual Explorer uses imagery in a process of dialogue to provide a language that doesn't belong to any one person but is shared among diverse people. The grammar of this third language is one of metaphors, intuitions, images, and emotions, and it helps create a bridge across which people can connect, despite their differences. Under its empowering capacity for communication, even subjects previously deemed undiscussable can be expressed as intuitions, emotions, and new ideas.

When Should Visual Explorer Be Used?

Groups are often adept at working with the data in front of them. However, it's what's *not* obvious that's the problem. Visual Explorer should be used when a situation is complex and has unknown elements and hidden assumptions. Visual Explorer is especially useful when there are a variety of perspectives involved and a number of social boundaries to be spanned. Visual Explorer helps explore the territory of a challenge, and helps integrate different views into a coherent picture. VE is a right-brain complement to left-brain analysis. In general, Visual Explorer offers the most benefits when a group has objectives such as the following:

- seeking patterns in complex issues and making connections
- seeking a variety of perspectives
- asking new questions
- eliciting stories and creating metaphors
- tapping into personal experiences and passions
- articulating what is known to the group
- creating or practicing dialogue
- building on ideas
- surfacing and channeling emotions and intuitions
- exploring the landscape of a complex set of issues
- imagining alternatives
- sparking humor and playfulness

In the following paragraphs, we describe some situations in which Visual Explorer has helped groups address their questions and challenges.

Seeking fulfilling work. During an exit interview, an employee reported to the company's human resources department that there were communication and morale problems within the company's production department. In an effort to get a reading on the group, the production manager used Visual Explorer during a staff meeting. After distributing the images around the room, he asked each person to pick an image that might help answer the following question: What is standing in my way to a fulfilling career or to being happy in the production department? The group generated a list of core issues and several action items. Several department members reported that it was one of the best discussions the group had participated in.

Balancing analysis with intuition. During a departmental business-planning session, a group was required to process an immense amount of data and data-driven analysis throughout the day. The group used Visual Explorer toward the end of the planning meeting to balance the analytical approach with an intuitive one. Group members approached the Visual Explorer session with either one of two key questions: (1) What have we overlooked? or (2) What do we need to pay attention to that we haven't already? The Visual Explorer session confirmed some of the group's deeply held values and provided a surge of energy at the end of a tiring strategic session. Group members felt more connected to their values in a profound and intuitive way, which helped them renew their commitment toward the plan they had developed.

Stories of past and future. In planning a retreat for the group she managed, a team leader decided to feature storytelling—she wanted to reveal the rich history behind the group's work that the newer members didn't know much about. She also wanted the group to tell stories about where it was going and what its future might look like. She began the retreat using Visual Explorer, asking each person to select three images: one connected to the past, one to the present, and one to the future. She also asked each person to pick among a set of images that had been turned facedown, but not to look at the image. She saved those pictures until later, when group members turned them over and asked themselves, "How might we get blindsided?"

Building the creative team. A manager for a group of engineers was trying to help the group achieve its goal of becoming more creative as a team. He began by encouraging the group to appreciate its strengths. He asked the team members to bring to a staff meeting a memento or something they made that represented the moments when they were at their creative or artistic best. At that meeting each team member picked a Visual Explorer image that stood for what their manager described as "the creative strengths or highlights of our group." The next day, the group manager noticed that many of the mementos and images had found a place on desks and office walls. There they served as signs that this group of engineers had reconnected their creativity to their individual talents.

Designer's Tip

Visual Explorer is flexible enough to use with small and large groups. But it can also generate insightful interludes during personal conversations. For example, our colleagues Al Selvin and Aldo de Moor used it when they met for the first time in a year at a railway station. Using the images to spur their responses, each asked the other, "How has life been for you?"

Figure 2. The playing-card size Visual Explorer supports a one-to-one interaction.
©2014 Center for Creative Leadership.

Why Should Visual Explorer Be Used?

As life in organizations gets more complex and faster paced, it gets harder to create and maintain shared understanding about the challenges at hand and how to respond. Visual Explorer helps create this shared understanding within a group by means of a process known as mediated dialogue (Palus & Drath, 2001). The word *dialogue* in this sense refers to a way of having conversations in which people attempt to get at the roots of what they assume and believe. That kind of conversation sets the stage for making better decisions and taking more effective actions. It also shifts the practice of leadership from the "person in charge" to a practice that is shared and owned by the group—people talking, thinking, and acting together in the face of their complex challenges to create shared direction, alignment, and commitment.

Group conversations are often necessary to meet an organizational challenge, but not all conversations rise to the level of a dialogue. One reason is that talk directed toward an end often depends too heavily on analysis and verbal acuity. Another problem is that when talking about controversial issues the message can get confused with the messenger. Visual Explorer helps circumvent these problems by "putting something in the middle" so that ideas that arise in the conversation are projected onto and from the images rather than the speakers. Visual Explorer enables people to disconnect from their own values, assumptions, and points of view for a moment yet stay engaged in the ensuing conversation. Because the images are new to the group, they carry no history and can form a neutral, safe territory for talk—a necessary component for elevating conversation to dialogue. The result is that, during a Visual Explorer session, people are less constrained by language and entrenched opinions, and are more able to perceive, handle, and create ideas.

To conduct an effective Visual Explorer session, it's not necessary for you to understand all of the theory and research behind it. Rarely is there a need to explain any of this background during a session. However, it may be helpful to consider what competencies and capabilities Visual Explorer enables during its use. Authors Charles Palus and David Horth have identified six creative leadership competencies that enable group members to create sense together in the face of complex

INSIGHT BEYOND SIGHT

CCL colleague Steadman Harrison had prepared a Visual Explorer session as part of Kenya's Nakuru Leadership Workshop when he was introduced to Enos, a man representing an advocacy group for Kenyan Disabled Citizens. As it happens, *Enos was blind*. Mindful that the session should accommodate the needs of all its participants, Steadman promptly assured him that he could be fully involved in the exercise. He asked Enos to briefly describe his organizational challenge and ideal future state (the session's two framing questions). Steadman then guided him around the room and briefly described each picture. To Steadman's surprise, the tour didn't take long. When he described an image of a donkey with its feet tied together, Enos exclaimed that this was just the picture he was looking for. When Steadman described another image as "a bird with outstretched wings having just caught a fish," Enos said that was his future organization. As Steadman tells the story, the richest part of the experience was watching Enos's sheer delight as each of the members of his small group described the two pictures in detail. Enos tearfully acknowledged what a great gift it was to be a part of such a wonderful exercise, which captured the challenges facing the disabled people of East Africa and the hope that he had for a day when so many people in need would have the resources to soar like eagles.

challenges (2002). Each of the six skills is evident during a typical Visual Explorer session.

Paying attention. Visual Explorer helps groups and their members develop the discipline of temporarily slowing down in order to look closely at a complex situation while using more channels of perception and using them more effectively.

Personalizing. Using Visual Explorer, groups and their members tap into unique life experiences and passions to provide insight and perspective on shared challenges.

Imaging. Visual Explorer sessions use the power of images, metaphors, and storytelling to create and communicate shared understanding of complex organizational challenges.

Serious play. Visual Explorer helps groups and their members generate knowledge through play of a serious kind—exploration, experimentation, bending rules and testing limits, levity, and sport. The dialogue sessions are typically a lot of fun, and yet quickly move the conversation to the level of underlying assumptions.

Collaborative inquiry. Visual Explorer sessions help groups and organizations have productive dialogue in addressing complex issues across the functional, hierarchical, demographic, and cultural boundaries found in organizations.

Crafting. Visual Explorer supports efforts for synthesizing issues, objects, events, and actions into integrated and meaningful results.

Who Can Conduct a Visual Explorer Session?

Most managers and many group members can successfully facilitate a basic Visual Explorer session. In most cases, it suffices to follow the instructions in this facilitator's guide and to provide some basic directions to the participants. The facilitator's job is simple and unobtrusive: to support a good conversation among the group members. That job usually requires only a beginner's level of facilitation skill. Beyond this, the facilitator needs only the skills that match the purpose of the Visual Explorer session. For example, to conduct strategic planning, the group needs a facilitator with some experience in leading a strategic-planning session. For Visual Explorer sessions that may surface conflict, a facilitator who can handle conflict is essential. Experienced hands at organizational change are needed when Visual Explorer is used in a long-term transformation initiative. These are just a few of the specialized situations in which facilitative skill in other areas can combine with Visual Explorer facilitation to create a productive environment for dialogue and problem solving.

Preparing for Visual Explorer

Visual Explorer works in a wide variety of contexts, either as a stand-alone tool or as part of a larger group process that employs other developmental activities that address an issue or challenge. To use Visual Explorer within a larger design, it's effective to place the Visual Explorer session in the middle of the design. For example, you might plan a three-part session as follows:

Review and Frame: Direct the group to revisit or experience the issue firsthand or to review key information about the challenge. Create the framing question(s).

Select and Share: Conduct the Visual Explorer session.

Review and Reflect: Analyze and refine the perspectives and ideas that emerge and then appropriately conclude the session.

You can conduct this sequence during a staff meeting, for example, or during a group retreat or as part of a developmental program.

Creating Effective Framing Questions

Effective framing questions are the key to a successful Visual Explorer session. An effective framing question is one that elicits the right conversation. The right conversation (in most situations) is one that is open, insightful, and honest; it gets down to the essence of the challenge or topic at hand. The wrong conversation is one in which people converse about a topic they don't find important or in which people remain closed to each other.

The first guideline for creating an effective framing question is to determine what the group wants or needs to explore. The group or the client for whom the group is working is the source for the most meaningful questions. Compose a few alternative ways to ask the framing questions, and then try them out with one or more of the participants before the session. You may be surprised at how a question can be interpreted differently from what you had in mind.

Good framing questions speak directly and honestly to the issues the participants care about. Good framing questions also draw participants into their own personal perspectives and experiences. Questions that are too general encourage vague responses, but questions that are specific to the issue and to the participant drive the conversation to deeper levels. Asking "How do *you* see [this issue]?" is better than asking "What is the most important aspect of [this issue]?"

Following are some sample framing questions. Rephrase them in terms of your own context. Often the use of two or three related questions is effective (for example, What is my greatest hope for this project? What is my greatest fear for this project?).

- What will success look like?

- What are the possibilities in our situation?

- How will the world look different as the result of my/our work? What will be my/our legacy?

- Personal reflection questions include the following: What defines me as a leader? What are my main contributions to this organization? What do I want in my career? What is my biggest aspiration? What do I want my legacy to be?

- What stood out for me in the data we just reviewed? What's most puzzling about this data or feedback?

- What strengths do I bring to this team? What "superpowers" do I bring to this team?

- What do I think we are missing, neglecting, or underestimating?

- What do I think the group is doing right? What are the group's strengths? How would I describe where the group has been? How would I describe where the group is going? What should our aspirations be?

- How would we do this if we had unlimited resources? What if we had no resources?

The following checklist will help you prepare for the most typical kinds of Visual Explorer sessions. For nontypical or special Visual Explorer sessions, turn to this manual's **Visual Explorer Applications** section for ideas on how to usefully adapt the tool's standard design and facilitation.

 Who will participate in the Visual Explorer session? Will you have the right people in the room?

 Why are you using Visual Explorer? How will you briefly describe the benefits for this particular group?

 Do you have a minimum of sixty minutes set aside for the session? Do you have enough time to get the benefits you want?

 Do you have the set of Visual Explorer images at your disposal? One set of images is typically enough for about twenty-four people. The more framing questions you ask, the more images you need to provide for browsing.

 What size images will you use? Letter-size images (8½ by 11 inches) have the strongest visual and emotional impact; they also require space (floor or table-top) to spread them out for browsing. The postcard-size images and playing-card-size images can be browsed in smaller spaces, even by thumbing if you don't have space to lay them out.

 Do you have enough space to spread out the images so that participants can browse through them? If you need some help with arranging the images for browsing (which can be done in a few minutes at the time of the session, or in advance), make sure to recruit an assistant.

Can chairs be moved so that small groups can face each other in clusters without tables? "Knee to knee" works very well, as people lean in to converse and share images.

 Will you assign a note taker to record the session dialogue? Notes can be shared after the session, or you can use some kind of groupware or presentation software to project the discussion in real time on a shared display. If you don't have a note taker, will you make an audio or video recording of the session? (Always discuss this with participants at the start, and make sure any ground rules for confidentiality are explicit.)

 What framing questions will you use? How might you pose better framing questions? Can the group state their own questions?

 If the session is part of a larger initiative, does the overall agenda continue the dialogue as a way to explore options surfaced during the session?

 Will the group use the images it selects and its discussion notes to communicate outcomes to stakeholders inside and outside the organization?

 Optional. Will you use a worksheet or journal for participants to record their reflections and notes? Will you be able to collect or copy that material for analysis and reflection by the group after the session?

 Optional. Will you play music for parts of the session? You will need a music player, instrumental (nonvocal) music, and adequate speakers.

Some framing questions and responses may initially be off limits and undiscussable in a group (Argyris, 1994). People may avoid saying certain things in a dialogue because they are self-protective or defensive, assuming negative consequences if the topic is surfaced. Visual Explorer dialogues often allow what was previously undiscussable to enter the conversation. Using images to mediate the dialogue allows people to speak about such things more circumspectly, in terms of metaphors, symbols, and likenesses, rather than as statements of fact. Putting the image in the middle of the dialogue allows what was previously undiscussable to be projected onto the image (rather than onto oneself or others) and held at arm's length.

For example, in a health care organization we worked with, there was widespread fear of retribution if critical opinions were voiced. Yet this fear was never admitted in public, and the senior team was largely unaware of it or denied it. We used Visual Explorer to debrief climate survey data in which the fear became more visible. The framing question was "What stood out for you in the data we just reviewed?" Several of the images raised the issue of fear, and it became an important aspect of the debrief. We combined their words with the images and presented the combination to them as a slide show, which they shared with others in the organization (see Figure 3, page 24). All this led to more open and honest conversations about fear in the workplace.

Recently, a team of CCL facilitators worked with a forum of senior government ministers in Laos. The forum was focused on the importance of leadership and leadership development in the context of the country's severe challenges. Leadership, as a theme, does not find much open, public discussion because of its strong association with the ruling communist party. The framing question we used for the Visual Explorer session was "How would you describe leadership in your own organization to new employees?" Before we asked participants to pick an image that spoke to that question, we took a few minutes to model the process of sharing images with one another. Once they returned to their seats, we turned them loose. The room was very quiet at the start. Then came voices, then attentive eyes, then leaned-in shoulders, then animated conversation, and finally laughter. Visual Explorer helped make the undiscussable (namely, leadership) discussable. It helped the group to view leadership as something not just associated with senior politburo members, but as something relevant to all. Given the conference theme, "Leadership Concerns Us All," this demystifying process was a great outcome to achieve.

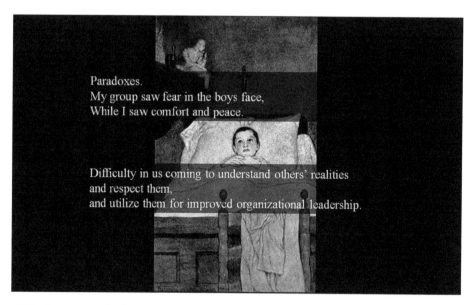

Figure 3. Visual Explorer can help groups get to matters that were previously off limits.
Photographs provided by Getty Images, Inc., ©2004. All Rights Reserved.

Conducting a Visual Explorer Session

A minimum of sixty minutes is usually required for a basic Visual Explorer session. Five steps constitute a typical session:

1. **Frame.** The first step is to identify the topic of the conversation and to focus it for the group with one or more framing questions. Time: variable.

2. **Browse.** Participants browse through all the images and choose one for each framing question. Time: 10 minutes.

3. **Reflect.** Participants quietly observe and think about the images and consider their responses to the question(s). Time: 10 minutes.

4. **Share.** Participants share their images one at a time and converse about the framing questions in connection with the images they've selected. Each person responds to each other's images. Time: at least 5 minutes per person.

5. **Extend.** After a Visual Explorer session there is often momentum for continuing the dialogue and doing something more with the insights. Groups often cascade the conversation to other stakeholders inside and outside the organization, using the selected images for further communications. Time: variable.

Step-by-Step Instructions

Frame. First, select the general topic of the conversation. For some groups the topic will be a given—for example, "It's about stating our vision." Some groups may need to consider a specific topic that is timely, relevant, and likely to lead to a fruitful conversation—for example, "What has it been like to be part of this team over the past year?" The team or group leader or facilitator may want the group to dig deeper into the issues at hand—for example, "What stands out as this group's key challenge?" or "What are the root causes of the problem that this group faces?" Consider making these or other approaches the agenda of a meeting prior to the Visual Explorer session, when the group or a part of the group can explore a range of possible topics and then choose one as the focus.

Next, create one or more framing questions based on the topic. These are the specific questions posed to the group that will guide their browsing and selection of images. For example, you could ask, "What do you think this group's new strategy should be? What will it look like in practice?" You can also put these issues in the form of framing statements—for example, "Pick an image that says something to you about what the group's new strategy should be."

How you develop and present the framing questions depends quite a bit on the nature of the group. Who is going to be in the room for the Visual Explorer session? Will each person find the framing questions meaningful? Is the group a collection of individuals, or is it an intact working team? The former might start with a question along the lines of "How am I creative?" The latter might add a second question, such as "How are we creative as a team?"

Using two or more framing questions to define the topic can be an effective facilitative tactic in that it pushes the group toward different conversations. For example, "What are our strengths as a team?" could be followed by "What could we improve as a team?" When each person picks an image of each, the conversation draws power from juxtaposing contrasting questions and images.

Now you're ready to present the activity to the group. You should anticipate two questions: "Why are we doing this activity?" and "What are the instructions?" For the former, it is best to say something simple and not overexplain or oversell the process. For example, "We are doing this to have an open and honest conversation about [your chosen topic]." Alternatively, you can answer, "We want to explore [your framing questions]." If the group is skeptical of Visual Explorer, ask them to try it as one of many tools available for looking more creatively at the issue at hand. Don't position it as a magic bullet. For the questions about instructions, you can refer to the numbered list above, or you may refer partici-

LEADERSHIP DEVELOPMENT AT A TELECOMMUNICATIONS COMPANY

CCL facilitators used Visual Explorer at a telecommunications company with a group of high-potential employees who were about to step into the executive ranks. They were invited to a leadership workshop to address a critical challenge the company faced: how to accelerate the cycle time for developing and introducing new products to the market. Facilitators asked each of the participants to choose an image that in some way provided a metaphor for the issues they were wrestling with in their part of the organization. Next, the participants shared their insights with the company's senior leadership team. In the course of linking the outcomes of the Visual Explorer session with the perspectives of top management, the executives who participated in the activity developed strategic thinking capabilities that helped them effectively engage with senior executives who held strategy development responsibility. The process, empowered by Visual Explorer, enabled the participants to make a useful contribution to the organization's strategic development and gave them a clearer understanding of their own roles in executing the strategy.

pants to the Visual Explorer Quick Guide, which you can find at the start of this manual. You may photocopy the Quick Guide to hand out to interested participants.

This is a good time to state any norms regarding the privacy of the group's conversations. Some groups may abide by the maxim of "What is said in the room stays in the room." Other groups may be more willing to go public with their experience.

An optional activity, reflection, can be used at this point before moving to the next step. Each person takes a few moments to write or reflect about his or her personal perspective on the topic and the framing question(s). These notes might include observations, ideas, further questions, emotions, points of confusion, and so on. Assure participants that these notes are private, but point out that they can be used to guide the selection of an image and can also be shared as a point of view during the session. Although this activity is optional, it can be effective in helping people to switch mental gears into a more reflective and attentive mode.

Browse. The second step in a Visual Explorer session occurs when participants browse through the images. The facilitator spreads out the pictures so they can be easily viewed by people as they walk around. Or you might provide one deck for each small group and let them spread the cards out among themselves. Typically, the images are placed on the floor or tabletops or both—wherever you have room. Some facilitators line them up neatly, and some like to scatter them more loosely—the arrangement doesn't matter as long as participants can easily reach any images that capture their attention. You can lay out the images before the session in a room separate from where you're conducting the session, or you can even use a hallway. In our experience, something develops—a kind of bemused camaraderie—between the participants as they jostle about. If you don't have an assistant, you can enlist the help of some of the participants to put the pictures out for browsing.

This step in the Visual Explorer process draws on the nonverbal right side of the brain—the part that processes patterns, intuitions, and emotions. Therefore, ask participants not to talk as they browse. If you like, you can play instrumental, upbeat music in the background.

Tell the participants to browse the images until they find one that relates to their answers or reactions to the framing question. The connection that they make can be of almost any kind—literal, rational, emotional, intuitive, symbolic, or otherwise. Tell the participants that they might not even know at first why they pick a particular image. Remind them to keep the framing question in the back of their minds and to relax, browse, and choose. Allow at least ten minutes and as long as people need.

In the browsing phase, even the skeptics begin to enjoy the process. The images are provocative. Browsing is a relaxed but alert state. People often experience connections to emotions and intuitions. Conscious, rational responses to the framing questions start rolling around with unformed and unarticulated responses. Metaphors suggest themselves. Sometimes, participants report, the choice of an image doesn't feel like

The resident consultant-trainer at a large, U.S.-based insurance and financial institution used Visual Explorer for team building within work groups. The tool's images helped build trust and alignment among and between teams. "It's not unusual for individuals in a work group—even those that have been together for a long time—to be ill at ease with each other," the company's trainer told us. "Using photos and images brings safety. You're not talking about me. Instead, you're talking about a picture. That's safer and inspires confidence."

a decision at all: "The image picked me," they say. Multiple meanings abound for any one image. The power of Visual Explorer is in this fluidity of multiple meanings in a highly visual context.

An option in the browsing phase is to use some of the images facedown. While you spread the pictures for browsing, turn a few of them over (at least one for each person participating) to hide the picture. As participants select images, ask them to also select one of the hidden ones but not to look at it. Near the end of the group conversations, participants will be able to look at the hidden image and respond. At that point ask them, "What if this image portrays what is missing . . . or neglected . . . or overlooked? What connection can you draw from the image?" Curiosity runs high about the hidden images. Even if most group members don't get any insights from the hidden pictures, a few will. Don't try to control the discussion, but be aware that it may provide an opening to issues that the group had previously avoided. Don't treat this as mystical—it's better to treat the hidden images as fun and serious play from which serious insights might arise.

Reflect. Although presented here as the third step in the process, reflection ideally occurs at several points during a Visual Explorer session: before and after browsing and at the end of the conversations. To encourage participants during this stage, tell them to spend some time looking at the images they've picked. Ask them to write down a few notes about what they see. You might prompt them as follows:

- Describe the scene in the picture.

- Describe any actions in the picture.

- Note what is unknown or vague about the picture.

- Think about and record why you are drawn to that image.

- Write down how the image connects to the framing question.

A more structured option is to hand out a worksheet on which participants can take notes and make reflections at the desired points in the process (for an example, see the Visual Explorer Worksheet on page 106).

Some facilitators or groups are tempted to skip or hurry this step. The outcome of the Visual Explorer session is enhanced when the facilitator holds people in this attentive state and they take time to explore the image they've selected. Challenge them to really look at what is in front of them, to move beyond first impressions. This is another step in which not talking can aid participants in paying close attention.

Share. With images selected and in hand, participants now share their images with each other and converse about the topic and questions. You can manage the time spent in this stage by breaking the large group into small groups with three to five people in each one. You can randomly assign people to the small groups, build groups as people finish browsing, put together people who don't know each other as well, or deliberately create diverse groups in whatever way fits your definition of diversity. Allow at least five minutes per person in each group. Let the groups know at the start how much time they have and keep them informed about their time throughout the process.

Make a simplified version of the following steps available to the group on a flip chart or as a handout or slide. It can be helpful to briefly demonstrate the steps wth an assistant in front of the group. As facilitator, you should let the groups manage themselves using some version of these instructions. You can move among the groups to help as needed.

The group sits in a circle, preferably without a table. Instruct participants that, as they carry out the task, they should refrain from solving problems for each other. They should not give or ask for advice. They should keep their attention on the images, questions, and answers. They should use the conversation to explore multiple perspectives and possible meanings. The first person shares his or her image(s) in a three-step manner as follows:

1. Share the image and describe the image itself (forget about any connection to the question for a moment). What is it? What is happening? What do you notice?

2. What connections do you make from the image to the question? How is the image a response to the question? (If the first person has more than one image, these two steps are repeated for each one.)

3. Each person in the group responds to the image(s) offered by the first person. Each response may consist of two parts.

   a. What do you see in the image? Do you see the same things that others see? What stands out to you?

   b. What connections do you make from the image to the question?

After the first person has shared his or her images with the group in this way, he or she can thank the group. The conversation moves on to the next person and his or her image(s). Continue until everyone has shared his or her images.

As time permits, allow groups to continue talking after the last person has shared images and to discuss patterns and themes and implications. The facilitator's role is to remain available to answer questions about the Visual Explorer process but not to exert too much control over the groups. It's all right if the groups slightly modify or improvise on the instructions. As they finish the sharing step, group members should make notes about insights from the conversation, including any shifts in perceptions, insights, or feelings about the topic. (The Visual Explorer Worksheet on page 106 may be used for this purpose.)

Extend. After the initial round of conversations in the sharing stage, groups often want to extend the conversation in directions they find important and to cascade their insights onto other groups in their organizations. For example, the group may want to reuse the images that provoked the strongest responses as a platform for ongoing problem solving, invention, and communication. To take advantage of that momentum, the facilitator can debrief the activity and continue the conversations as desired. Here are some key questions to use while debriefing:

- How would you describe your conversation?
- What happened during your conversation?
- What was valuable about the whole process, from browsing to sharing?
- What did you discover about [the topic] from your group?
- What different points of view were expressed in the small groups?
- Which images really stood out in your small group? Which stand out to the entire group?

Options for enhancing your Visual Explorer session. Within the basic sequence just described, facilitators can do several things to make the session even more useful to participants after they conclude the session.

Keep Tabs: Record or transcribe the discussions, preserving the metaphors, the insights, and the images for future reference. For example, the images can be taped to white paper on an easel or wall and annotated with text. Figure 4 shows a diagram created around the framing question, "What is our purpose?"

Make History: Save the images to use as prompts when the group reconvenes. The images can be photocopied or scanned. For example, a newly formed team participating in a Visual Explorer session listed all the metaphors that surfaced during the dialogue that described their mission. It used this list to refine and communicate its mission to outside sponsors, and among its own members.

Rank and File: Prioritize the most interesting connections or insights. Do any of them suggest specific actions or next steps? For example, another organization using Visual Explorer took input from a number of sessions and used that as a starting point for a vision statement.

Cut, Collect, Create: Use scissors, glue, poster paper, markers, and additional images from magazines and other sources to construct a collage—a composite representation of the topic—using the Visual Explorer images selected. The collage, in turn, can become an object that spurs further dialogue.

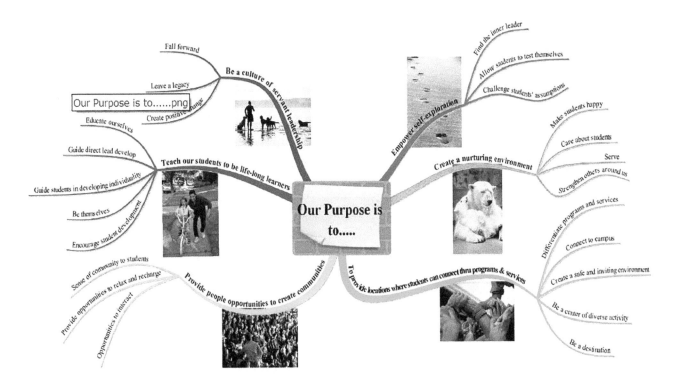

Figure 4. Mapping ideas from a Visual Explorer session. *Source: Bruce Flye.*

In the years that CCL facilitators and coaches, team leaders, consultants, organization development staffs, and others have conducted Visual Explorer sessions, they have generated a number of tips and best practices. Following are some ideas that will give facilitators at all skill levels confidence and encouragement for putting Visual Explorer to use in their organizations and with their clients.

Just Do It: In many cases Visual Explorer runs itself. People are natural storytellers and image readers.

Test It: Try Visual Explorer in some low-key situations with two or three people before trying it in a complex situation.

Don't Overexplain: When you facilitate a Visual Explorer session, don't talk too much about the tool or the theories behind it. Don't micromanage the process. A simple, brief demonstration of how to share the images (using just one image and two people) can be helpful.

Use the Wow Factor: People tend to really enjoy looking at the images. Especially when spread around a room, the set of pictures is inviting, attractive, and provocative. People get drawn into the process even if they are skeptical.

Make Choosing Magical: The magic of choosing is what participants feel when they have the time and relaxed freedom to browse randomly and then choose an interesting and meaningful image. *Sometimes the image picks you!* Compare that experience to one in which people are asked challenging questions directly in ways that can put them on the defensive.

Allow Adequate Time: Don't hurry. Visual Explorer creates periods of slow, careful attention and reflection, and periods of dynamic conversation. While we have seen Visual Explorer used effectively as a brainstorming tool, its depth and power are fully realized when participants can slow down and really look at the images in front of them.

Encourage Silence: Selecting images is an intuitive, emotional, spatial activity; words get in the way. Gently remind people not to chat as they're selecting their images. Feel free to play some instrumental, upbeat, nonintrusive music in the background.

Ask the Right Framing Questions: The quality of the framing questions impacts the quality of image selection and the subsequent dialogue. Good framing questions speak directly and honestly to the issues the participants care about. Good framing questions tend to draw participants into their own personal perspectives and experiences.

Offer Reflection Time: Writing (journaling or jotting notes) can focus the Visual Explorer session and provide participants with a record of their experience, to which they can return periodically for further reflection.

Use the Right Number of Images: Some facilitators find that the full set of images contains too many pictures. If the space available for your session precludes spreading out the full set or if you have a small number of participants, you can get by with fewer pictures. You can cut the number of images by removing some at random or by choosing to remove those that are the least resonant with the framing questions.

Capture Everything Digitally: Text from the session can be preserved and combined with the digital images with stunning results. A simple digital camera can capture the images themselves as well as visual artifacts (like flip charts) created during the session. Multimedia knowledge mapping software like Compendium can be used very effectively (Selvin, Shum, Horth, Palus, & Sierhuis, 2002).

Visual Explorer Applications

In this section, we introduce a variety of specific ways in which Visual Explorer can be applied. Visual Explorer has a powerful versatility that allows facilitators to generate creative conversations, to precipitate appreciative inquiry, to foster collaborative dialogue, and to develop leadership capacity. It has been used extensively in one-on-one coaching, and even as a personal reflection tool.

Each application treatment begins with a short introduction to the use of Visual Explorer in that specific context. We list benefits to using Visual Explorer in that way. To encourage further experiments using Visual Explorer, we also describe related applications. What we call Facing Complex Challenges, for example, is related to Creative Problem Solving and to Visioning. Facilitators can cross-pollinate applications to customize and invent their own scenarios for the use of Visual Explorer. We encourage you to share your ideas and experiences with us (send to ccllabs@ccl.org) for posting, with your permission, on the Visual Explorer blog—you can find the URL in this guide's References and Resources section.

Further, we provide instructions for facilitating a Visual Explorer session in each particular context, and we provide an example of the application in action. Finally, we provide a list of additional resources that can help facilitators think more deeply about and act with greater purpose and precision in regard to each application. Full bibliographic information for the additional application resources is located in this guide's References and Resources pages.

Benefits of This Application

- Provokes new questions
- Generates alternatives
- Builds direction, alignment, and commitment
- Builds on ideas
- Articulates what has been unspoken or is undiscussable
- Encourages fun, playful, yet serious dialogue
- Taps into personal experiences and passions
- Draws careful attention to details and to the big picture
- Makes abstract conversations tangible
- Helps frame and illustrate thoughts so they can be shared
- Surfaces individual and group assumptions
- Bridges different contexts and cultures
- Creates new metaphors
- Helps individuals and groups get unstuck

Dialogue is a skilled conversation that invites shared meaning-making and deeper inquiry. By putting images in the middle of a dialogue, Visual Explorer helps groups surface and explore assumptions and perspectives, so that they can be more collaborative, innovative, and effective in the longer term. "Slowing down now to speed up later" is a key proposition of dialogue. Visual Explorer supports dialogue by providing a safe and reliable way for people to constructively apply their emotions, intuitions, opinions, insights, and personal experiences in service of the challenges at hand.

Facilitation

In using Visual Explorer to generate dialogue, the basic instructions in this guide for a typical Visual Explorer session apply. Facilitators should note the following points if serious, long-term dialogue is a goal of the group.

- Prior experience with Visual Explorer is helpful.

- Skill in facilitating dialogue is necessary if the conditions for talking at this level of engagement are difficult or risky.

- Dialogue is a process that occurs over time and can't be limited to an hour-long session. What happens before and after the Visual Explorer session will determine the quality of the long-term relationships among the participants. For this reason, a basic level of trust must be present. Facilitators can design follow-on activities to take advantage of deepening trust and relationships.

- Do not shortcut the sharing of images during the Visual Explorer session if dialogue is the

Dialogue is the foundational application of Visual Explorer, and the basis for the other applications. While it is true that Visual Explorer can be used in many other ways, it is the potential for deeper levels of engagement that makes Visual Explorer such an effective tool. The dialogue pointers in this section thus have value for all the other applications.

goal. Paying careful attention to the images each person selects—from his or her perspective and from the perspective of others—can move the participants past superficial interactions.

- Visual Explorer can surface strong emotions and powerful insights, and it can shine a light on topics assumed to be off limits. The facilitator should allow for enough time, for a safe space, and for adequate exploration and follow-up to do justice to the powerful experience created for at least some of the participants.

- The right-brain (visual, nonverbal, intuitive) aspects of Visual Explorer are very helpful to dialogue. Emphasize not talking during the browsing, play instrumental music, and allow time for the right-brain thought processes to kick in. Encourage people to slow down and pay attention to the details of the images—not thinking about the challenge at first, but just looking at the images themselves. Journaling and reflecting also support right-brain cognition.

Example of This Application in Action

The senior leadership team at Angstrom Inc., a telecommunications company, met one weekend to think about business strategy in the face of significant challenges. The team talked with a number of invited experts, who presented their views of a rapidly changing telecom industry. After the experts had their say, the team wanted a deeper dialogue to make shared sense of what they had just heard. Visual Explorer was used to help the team reflect amid this flood of information. The Visual Explorer session focused on this framing question: "What stands out above all else from this morning's presentations, and why?"

The team broke into groups of three or four. Each group shared its images among its members and generated plenty of insights. The Visual Explorer session began a cycle of dialogue that ran throughout the day and that the team used to imagine the company's future. For example, one team member, John, selected a picture of a person ice-fishing (see Figure 5). John used the image to describe the simplicity and the demands of fishing. Angstrom is a high-tech business, yet for John, the work came down to certain basics: patience, focus, and a bit of suffering. John's small group noticed in his picture the wooden stick and simple metal tool lying on the ice and tried to determine what those represented in Angstrom's business. They noticed that the person in the picture was alone, and they wondered why.

Figure 5. One participant reads simplicity in this image.
Photographs provided by Getty Images, Inc., ©2004. All Rights Reserved.

Additional Resources for This Application

Bohm. *On Dialogue.*

Dixon. *Perspectives on Dialogue.*

Dixon. *Dialogue at Work.*

Ernst & Yip. "Boundary Spanning Leadership."

Isaacs. "Basic Components of a Dialogue Session."

Kahane. *Solving Tough Problems.*

McGuire & Palus. "Using Dialogue as a Tool for Better Leadership."

McGuire & Rhodes. *Transforming Your Leadership Culture.*

Palus & Drath. "Putting Something in the Middle."

Palus & Horth. *The Leader's Edge.*

Schrage. *Serious Play.*

Schwartz. *The Art of the Long View.*

Vogt, Brown, & Isaacs. *The Art of Powerful Questions.*

Another team member, Mary, chose an image of a rock climber (see Figure 6). She talked about the exhilaration and fear she experienced working at Angstrom. Another member of her group noticed that Mary held the image upside down—the trees in the distance belonged at the bottom. The conversation shifted to examine perspectives, and the group began a dialogue about what might happen if certain key assumptions that Angstrom held were inverted.

Figure 6. Exhilaration and fear combine in another participant's image. *Photographs provided by Getty Images, Inc., ©2004. All Rights Reserved.*

> **Benefits of This Application**
>
> - Draws careful attention to details and to the big picture
> - Surfaces individual and group assumptions
> - Bridges different contexts and cultures
> - Creates new metaphors
> - Builds direction, alignment, and commitment
> - Helps individuals and groups get unstuck
> - Calls forth artistry
> - Enables a shared understanding that helps in establishing a vision, making decisions, creating action steps, and picturing impacts
> - Surfaces, engages, and transcends emotional undercurrents

Complex challenges sprawl in many directions, across many territories. It's hard to see them clearly, yet it requires many perspectives to see them at all. Too often, technical fixes are applied, ineffectively, before the problem is seen and understood in its totality as well as its detail. Complex, adaptive challenges (Heifetz, 1994) are beyond technical fixes. Leadership has to come from the community of members and stakeholders, integrating and applying their shared knowledge. Intelligent transformation, rather than only incremental change, is the expected result of community-level engagement of complex challenges (Palus, Horth, Selvin, & Pulley, 2003).

"Sensemaking" is what people do in the rush of complex events to comprehend and anticipate what is happening to them (Kelly, 1955; Weick, 1995). Amid complexity and near chaos, it is key to ask, answer, and reanswer "What is this? What is happening to us now?" This kind of sensemaking is largely a social process. It is a matter of debating and sometimes agreeing about what is familiar and unfamiliar, of naming things, of discerning patterns. Competent sensemaking provides the foundation for committed action. It becomes a core capability in the "making common sense" process of shared leadership (Drath & Palus, 1994). Visual Explorer is a tool for sensemaking. It helps groups of people pay careful attention to the challenge, from multiple perspectives, using visual and metaphoric modes of perception and insight.

Visual Explorer is especially useful at the front end of an action learning process, as the challenge is first discovered and explored (perhaps in various teams) and a vision for its solution is established. The leader or coach of such teams should work to shift the ways in which

- Enabling dialogue
- Creative problem solving
- Visioning
- Appreciative inquiry
- Team coaching

the group pays attention to the challenge, and Visual Explorer can be an effective tool for enabling such shifts.

Facilitation

The coach or leader can introduce Visual Explorer as a process for engaging the challenge such that maximum input and multiple viewpoints are sought up front. Instructions for the five basic steps of a typical Visual Explorer session apply, with additional emphasis put on capturing and reusing key insights from the Visual Explorer session in crafting a long-term solution to the challenge. For example, a session might have three framing questions: "What does this challenge look and feel like to us now? What will a sustainable solution to this challenge look like in the future? What will it look like to move from now to the future?"

Example of This Application in Action

Verizon formed action learning teams of high-potential director-level managers. Each team focused for eight weeks on a complex challenge of its own selection. At the start of this process, each team member used Visual Explorer to explore his or her own complex challenge and relate it to those of peers. In this way the shared aspects of their individual challenges would emerge to become the focus of the action learning teams.

Managers were asked to browse the Visual Explorer images (all laid faceup in the hallway) and select two: "one which stands for, literally, or metaphorically, or emotionally, or intuitively, the way your challenge is now and one which stands for what the path forward with your challenge might be like."

Participants then gathered in groups of four or five to have a dialogue about their challenges, using the images as mediating objects. A volunteer went first and started by describing her first image in detail: What is the image? What are the details? What is mysterious or surprising? Then (and not until then) that person described the challenge and how it connected with the image. This same volunteer did the same for her second image. Then the other persons in the group responded to that same image, first describing what they saw in the image, especially if they saw something different. Then the respondents made their own connections to the challenge the volunteer had described, using language of the form "If that were my image, I would connect it to your challenge like this . . . . What I notice in that image and the associations I have are . . . ." Advice and criticism were not allowed. Finally, the originator of the image "took back" the image with a concluding thought and a thank-you. The process proceeded with each person in turn placing his or her images and challenges in the middle of the dialogue.

The results of this exercise were positive. Comments afterward included the following:

- "Before we started, I was doubtful about the pictures, but then we were able to talk about our challenges in depth."

- "We came up with some metaphors we otherwise would not have. It seemed easy to tell stories to go with the images."

- "People in our group tended to see very different things in the same image—and that was okay."

- "It was fun. We laughed. The connections led to a lot of puns and jokes."

For example, consider one participant's initial challenge and then the way forward she saw: "How do we restructure to increase penetration of our largest customers in terms of becoming a true ICP?"

Additional Resources for This Application

Ackoff. *The Art of Problem Solving*.

Compendium Institute (Web site).

Conklin. *Dialogue Mapping*.

Drath & Palus. "Making Common Sense."

Ernst & Yip. *Boundary Spanning Leadership*.

Heifetz. *Leadership without Easy Answers*.

McGuire & Rhodes. *Transforming Your Leadership Culture*.

Palus & Horth. *The Leader's Edge*.

Palus, Horth, Selvin, & Pulley. "Exploration for Development."

Rimanoczy & Turner. *Action Reflection Learning*.

Selvin. "Performing Knowledge Art."

Selvin et al. "Compendium."

Weick. *Sensemaking in Organizations*.

She described an image (see Figure 7) she had selected as representative of the challenge this way: "This shows the building of a traditional brick structure—not flexible, people working at individual tasks, no collaboration. It has a static feel, with little or no movement. This represents our current environment—traditional products presented in a product-centric way, a standardized approach."

Figure 7. For one leader, this picture suggested a lack of flexibility in her company.
Photographs provided by Getty Images, Inc., ©2004. All Rights Reserved.

Alternatively, she described another image she had selected (see Figure 8) as speaking to a possible way ahead: "Taking flight into the air, with freedom, and a strong sense of movement. Physical touching represents a collaborative approach. There is a feeling of excitement and apprehension—and tension. This represents a non-standard approach to our largest customers—a requirement for flexibility, but based on strong training, skills, and expertise. We need to build these skills in the organization."

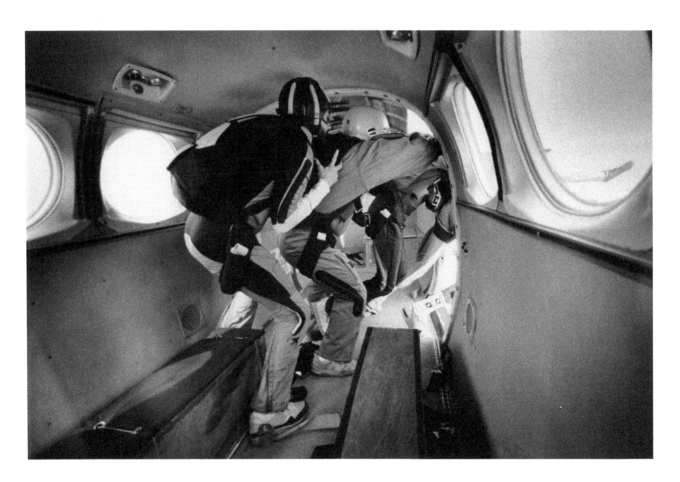

Figure 8. A combination of skill, training, and risk suggests a possible way forward.
Photographs provided by Getty Images, Inc., ©2004. All Rights Reserved.

Benefits of This Application

- Helps you assess who you are and where you are as a company in a marketplace
- Helps you scan your environment and your organization with fresh eyes
- Helps you explore, clarify, and communicate mission, vision, and values
- Helps identify key strategic drivers
- Surfaces ideas, intuitions, and new perspectives
- Helps individuals and groups get unstuck
- Surfaces, engages, and transcends emotional undercurrents

An important part of strategic thinking is visual, imaginative, intuitive, and nonlinear. Visual Explorer is a tool for supporting this often neglected part of strategic thinking. It supports strategy as a learning process, and can help clarify the strategic questions of who we are, where we are, and where we want to go.

Hughes and Beatty (2005) describe strategy as a learning process that makes use of rational as well as intuitive processes (see Figure 9 on following page). They describe Visual Explorer as a tool for "clearing the lens" of the strategic learning process—clarifying mission, vision, and values.

Facilitation

The five basic steps for a Visual Explorer session apply here, as well as the further measures suggested for enabling dialogue. It's useful to capture the key images, metaphors, and language from the Visual Explorer session as a means of engaging others in the strategic learning process.

Example of This Application in Action

Hughes and Beatty define strategic drivers as the "relatively few determinants of sustainable competitive advantage for a particular organization in a particular industry or competitive environment" (2005, p. 27). Bruce Byington, one of our colleagues at CCL, uses Visual Explorer to teach a process of strategic driver identification. These are the key steps in the process:

1. As a first step, Visual Explorer is used to bring out new ideas and help to "unstick" people and groups as they explore versions of some of the following framing questions:

- What industry or business are we in?
- What is our vision?
- What would real success look like?
- What are we missing that might surprise us?
- What is the key organizational capability we need to drive our strategy?

2. Brainstorm potential strategic drivers, as informed by the Visual Explorer dialogue.

3. Sort, classify, and prioritize potential drivers.

Related Applications

- Enabling dialogue
- Facing complex challenges
- Change leadership
- Creative problem solving
- Visioning
- Creating scenarios of the future
- Appreciative inquiry
- Individual coaching
- Team coaching

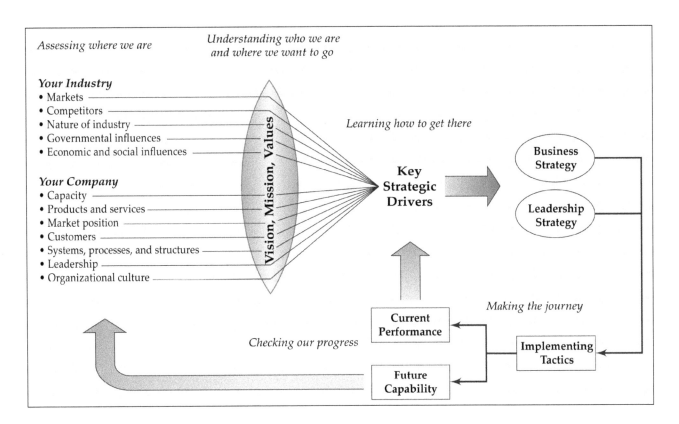

Figure 9. Strategy as a Learning Process

Additional Resources for This Application

De Kluyver. *Strategic Thinking.*

Hughes & Beatty. *Becoming a Strategic Leader.*

McGuire & Rhodes. *Transforming Your Leadership Culture.*

Mintzberg. "Crafting Strategy."

Palus & Horth. *The Leader's Edge.*

Palus & Horth. "Visual Explorer." In *The Change Handbook.*

Pasmore & Lafferty. *Developing a Leadership Strategy.*

Selvin. "Performing Knowledge Art."

Selvin et al. "Compendium."

Benefits of This Application

- Provokes new questions
- Generates alternatives
- Builds on ideas
- Encourages fun, playful, yet serious dialogue
- Builds direction, alignment, and commitment
- Clarifies and communicates mission, vision, and values
- Draws attention to details and to the big picture
- Surfaces individual and group assumptions
- Bridges different contexts and cultures
- Creates new metaphors
- Calls forth artistry
- Makes self-disclosure and vulnerability safe
- Taps into personal experiences and passions
- Helps individuals and groups get unstuck

Effective organizational change is often about transforming the culture. Such change requires leadership as well as management, and Visual Explorer, because of its ability to support dialogue in the face of complex challenges, is a useful tool for change leadership.

An important part of change leadership in large systems is what we call "taking it to the middle." This means engaging leaders across all parts of the organization, with special attention to the integrating power of the middle levels of management (Oshry, 2007). Whole-system dialogue using Visual Explorer at a retreat, at a program, or off-site can engage these diverse perspectives while helping to create a new shared direction, realignment, and renewed or revised commitments.

Facilitation

The use of Visual Explorer in change leadership and large-scale culture transformation requires substantial preparation and experience. Visual Explorer is merely a tool in such contexts, always used as part of a larger leadership strategy and extensive tool kit. The use of Visual Explorer in change contexts should generally follow the steps taken for creating dialogue, but adapted for large groups, across many gatherings.

Useful framing questions for change leadership include the following:

- What is our leadership culture now?
- What kind of leadership culture do we need in order to attain our vision, mission, and/or business strategy?
- How will we get from our present culture to our future culture?

- Enabling dialogue
- Facing complex challenges
- Strategic leadership
- Creative problem solving
- Visioning
- Creating scenarios of the future
- Appreciative inquiry
- Team coaching

- What does the path forward look like? Ideally? Actually?

- What should we keep in how we do things now? What should we change? Invent?

- Who are we at our best? Our worst?

Example of This Application in Action

Lenoir Memorial Hospital in Kinston, North Carolina, conducts change leadership in support of the ongoing transformation of their culture. Near the beginning of their change leadership initiative, a multiday whole-system retreat was held with the senior leadership team and broad representation of middle management. The purpose of the retreat was to "take it to the middle"—for senior management to fully engage the middle and the whole of the organization in leading change amidst significant organizational challenges.

On the second day of the retreat, an Open Space Forum (Owen, 1997) was run, in which the forty or so attendees clustered into groups around ten self-nominated issues. For example, one issue was "becoming the employer of choice in our community." After some initial discussion of the topic, each of the groups did a Visual Explorer session. For possible framing questions we suggested "What's most puzzling about this issue? What does it look like to you? What stands out?" Each group determined its own question. The participants completed a worksheet on which they stated the issue, reflected on the framing question, and then, after picking an image, described the image and its connection to the issue. After the Visual Explorer session, each group continued its open space conversations by writing up insights and action steps. The Visual Explorer sessions proved helpful in coalescing these insights across sometimes conflicting perspectives.

Afterward, a slide show was distributed that combined key words from the participants overlaid on the Visual Explorer images they chose (see Figure 10).

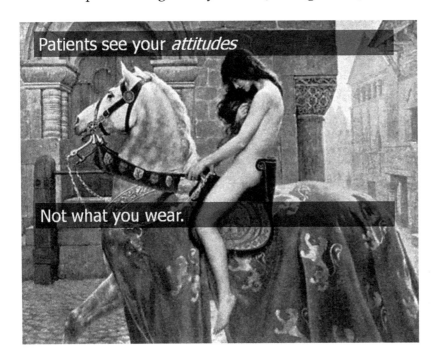

Figure 10. In this Visual Explorer session, participants captured insights that they incorporated into their images. *Photographs provided by Getty Images, Inc., ©2004. All Rights Reserved.*

Additional Resources for This Application

Cooperrider & Whitney. "Appreciative Inquiry."

Ernst & Chrobot-Mason. *Boundary Spanning Leadership.*

Hurst. *Crisis & Renewal.*

Kotter & Cohen. *The Heart of Change.*

McGuire & Rhodes. *Transforming Your Leadership Culture.*

Oshry. *Seeing Systems.*

Owen. *Open Space Technology.*

Palus, Horth, Selvin, & Pulley. "Exploration for Development."

Pasmore & Lafferty. *Developing a Leadership Strategy.*

Selvin & Palus. "Sensemaking Techniques in Support of Leadership Development."

Selvin et al. "Knowledge Art."

Benefits of This Application

- Encourages lateral thinking, new ideas, fresh connections, new metaphors, shared images
- Taps into personal experiences and passions
- Makes abstract conversations tangible
- Helps frame and illustrate thoughts so they can be shared
- Makes the invisible visible and the unconscious conscious
- Bridges different contexts and cultures
- Encourages sharing of perspectives in a way that leads to synthesis and the construction of new perspectives
- Elicits fresh, memorable metaphors and stories about complex challenges
- Enables understanding of emotions, intuitions, and tacit knowledge that might otherwise be left unspoken and undiscovered
- Produces tangible images that can be reused in paper and digital forms
- Surfaces ideas and new perspectives
- Helps individuals and groups get unstuck

Creative problem solving (CPS) embraces three principles: (1) everybody has creative ability, (2) widely varying types of creative ability are complementary, and (3) CPS consists of cycles of divergence, in which individuals cast a wide net employing lateral thinking, and convergence, when groups and individuals make judgments about the ideas and begin to focus on the problem at hand (Osborn, 1953; Parnes, 1992a). CCL developed an approach to targeted innovation based on CPS principles as a way of applying problem solving in the context of creative leadership (Gryskiewicz, 1999). Visual Explorer works well in CPS situations as a tool for imaginative thinking and insightful conversations.

For example, brainstorming is a type of idea generation that benefits from Visual Explorer. Brainstorming may appear easy—but it's hard to do well. The most common mistakes are limiting the depth and breadth of the ideas gathered. It's common for people to be conservative and cautious, especially around peers. Some groups express their ideas in analytical or expert ways. Sometime only a few people contribute and the rest hang back. One team leader describes it this way:

> In many of our projects and brainstorming sessions, it's still just a select few that are jumping out of the box and looking at things differently. People still revert back to their comfort zones, and revert back to incremental explanations as opposed to bold initiatives. I try to get them to ask, "Is there anything else missing?"

Visual Explorer can bypass these limits by allowing thoughts and feelings to be projected onto the image. The figurative, imaginative aspect is obvious and inviting to participants, and conducive to openness. People lose their fear about "saying the wrong thing." Ideas are channeled through the more visual-spatially oriented right brain, while the more judgmental and hair-splitting left brain is de-emphasized.

Facilitation

Each of the three parts that compose CPS (challenge exploration, idea generation, and preparation for action) entails a divergent phase that is followed by a convergent phase. Visual Explorer is effective for divergent thinking within all three parts of the creative problem-solving process, and it is especially beneficial during the challenge exploration and idea generation phases.

Challenge exploration. Complex challenges are messy. Often people are trying to solve the wrong problem, and they perceive and frame the challenge in terms of their past experience. Solutions to the wrong problem can increase the complexity and messiness of the challenge. Visual Explorer enables groups to step back from the challenge as originally framed, to gain new perspectives, and to reframe the challenge. Understanding the challenge, context, and goals within a new set of perceptions and assumptions can open up a broader range of possible solutions. It is a key step to getting new ideas and a fresh perspective on the right problem. As American educator John Dewey suggested, "A problem is half-solved if properly stated."

Before beginning the Visual Explorer session, it is useful to frame an initial challenge statement, a question about which the challenged individual or group wants to gather ideas. An effective challenge statement generates multiple perspectives and options on the complex challenge and steers away from messiness. Frame the challenge statement in the following way:

- Begin with an invitational stem, such as "How to . . ." or "In what ways might . . . ." Such phrases engage participants in generating options by allowing for uncertainty and avoiding the trap of premature convergence. Such stems facilitate new

- Enabling dialogue
- Facing complex challenges
- Strategic leadership
- Change leadership
- Visioning
- Creating scenarios of the future
- Individual coaching
- Team coaching
- Youth and young adult education
- Retreats and off-site meetings

perspectives on the complexity the individual or group faces.

- Identify the owner of the problem: "In what ways might **we** . . . ."

- Use an action verb: "In what ways might we **reduce** . . . ."

- Include the object, goal, or area of concern: "In what ways might we reduce **absenteeism** . . . ."

The statement should be free of criteria. Criteria promote convergent thinking prematurely. They shut down exploration and generation of productive ideas.

In the case of our example, which follows on the next page, you can use the initial challenge statement as the framing question for the Visual Explorer session: "How might we reduce absenteeism in our call centers?" Using the five-step Visual Explorer process, participants examine the challenge through its connection with the Visual Explorer images that each person selects, engaging in dialogue about assumptions, perceptions, and ideas pertaining to the challenge.

At the end of the Visual Explorer session, ask the group (or the challenge owner), "Considering the dialogue you just had, how satisfied are you with the initial challenge statement? Might there be better ways of framing the challenge?" If the answer is yes, then reframe the challenge with the group's input. The problem-solving group should generate at least a dozen new challenge statements (on a flip chart or with sticky notes) based on the insights from the Visual Explorer session. The owner of the challenge then selects those statements that seem to have the highest potential for generating solutions and shared commitment to those solutions. The selected statements can be used in turn to generate ideas for solution by using idea generation techniques (described in the next section).

The following examples suggest how new perceptions gained from a Visual Explorer session provide ways of reframing the challenge with a group. You might use these or similar reframing techniques if your group senses new, possible solutions to the problem but struggles to clarify them and put them into words.

To make a challenge statement *more general*:

- Initial framing: "How to improve the aluminum beverage can."

- Reframe: "How to design a functional beverage packaging system."

To *question assumptions* associated with the original challenge statement:

- Initial framing: "How to increase the speed of baseball players in reaching first base."

- Reframe: "Why speed? Maybe it is also a problem of lightness of equipment? Maybe better reaction time could make a difference? Why baseball players? Is this a problem for players of football, hockey, or other sports? Why first base? Is there not a problem in quickness in stealing bases, running for fly balls, and other tasks demanding speed?"

To *discern the components* of the challenge:

- Initial framing: "How to eliminate the tardiness of plant employees."

- Reframe: "How to motivate employees to arrive on time, how to make it easy to arrive on time, how to express the importance of punctuality."

To define *the real problem*:

- Initial framing: "How to redesign a fund-raising program for a university."

- Reframe: "How to convince graduates that money is needed, how to make money for the university, how to get rid of the current fund-raising committee."

To imagine *solutions without constraints*:

- Initial framing: "How to reduce the costs of the benefits program without reducing benefits."

- Reframe: "I wish benefits didn't cost so much, I wish we could manage the program without an administrative staff, I wish our people were healthier, I wish our insurance premiums didn't cost so much."

Idea generation. After the group has reframed a problem, it can begin to generate ideas for solving it. One brainstorming technique called Visual Connections (Geschka, 1990) illustrates how Visual Explorer images encourage idea generation. The steps outlined below can be used as a guide to running the Visual Connections exercise using Visual Explorer.

Step 1. Prior to the exercise, the facilitator selects four Visual Explorer images to show the group. Select images that

- evoke the senses (taste, sound, sight, smell, touch)

- elicit memories (grandmother's kitchen, for example, or school days)

- stimulate emotions (fear, joy, anger, or confusion, for example)

- differ from each other in most other ways

Sequence the four images as follows: (1) something with some mystery or a story in it, (2) something realistic and factual in nature, (3) something analytical or structural, and (4) something that readily evokes emotion.

Step 2. Instruct participants to write the challenge statement at the top of the Visual Connections Worksheet (photocopy the number of worksheets you need from the template found at the end of this application; see page 59).

Step 3. Show the first picture. Instruct the members of the group to record (under Image 1 on the worksheet) any sensory impressions, words, or reactions which come to mind when viewing the picture. Participants should work quickly and without speaking to get down immediate impressions. Show the image for two or three minutes, or until everyone has finished writing. Encourage participants to stay with the image longer than they might think is necessary, as if they are looking at an interesting artwork in a favorite gallery.

Step 4. Proceed in the same manner until all pictures have been shown and impressions recorded in the first column of the worksheet. In sequencing the four images, follow this rubric: from simple to complex, from passive to active, from absence of people to social complexity.

Step 5. Ask participants to consider the challenge statement again as they review what they have written for their impression of each image. For each set of impressions, they should make one or more connections or ideas related to the challenge statement and write these in the appropriate space on the worksheet. Encourage participants not to overthink, but to simply connect the impressions to the problem as defined by the challenge statement. The connections do not have to be practical or reasonable. Do this for each set of impressions.

Step 6. Ask each person to verbally share the impressions and connections he or she has recorded for the first image. The facilitator records all the connections on a flip chart or screen. Encourage participants to build on the ideas of others and to generate more connections. If time is short, you can decide not to go through all of the impressions for each image, or you can choose not to discuss all four pictures.

Step 7. At this point, the group has engaged in a lot of divergent exploration. The exercise now moves toward convergence. Ask the group to harvest and refine what it considers the most promising ideas. Label clusters of related ideas, and guide the group in restating the best ideas as precisely as it can. You may also need

Additional Resources for This Application

Ackoff. *The Art of Problem Solving.*

Amabile. *Growing Up Creative.*

Conklin. *Dialogue Mapping.*

Creative Education Foundation (Web site).

Edwards. *Drawing on the Artist Within.*

Geschka. "Visual Confrontation."

Gryskiewicz. *Positive Turbulence.*

Gryskiewicz & Taylor. *Making Creativity Practical.*

Isaksen, Dorval, & Treffinger. *Creative Approaches to Problem Solving.*

Osborn. *Applied Imagination.*

Parnes. *Source Book for Creative Problem Solving.*

Parnes. *Visionizing.*

Perkins. *The Intelligent Eye.*

Selvin. "Performing Knowledge Art."

Selvin et al. "Compendium."

to reframe and restate the challenge statement based on these new ideas. As a guide to facilitating this part of the process, consider this tactic: Give everyone in the group ten sticky dots or some other way to signify votes for the most promising idea clusters. Then the group can vote for the "hot spots" in the patterns the group sees: those clusters that spark energy, seem most plausible, create interesting work—or any pattern of ideas the group prefers.

Example of This Application in Action

Here is an example of successfully reframing a challenge statement using Visual Explorer as part of a larger creative problem-solving process. The Director of Service Centers for a telecommunications company is wrestling with high and ever-increasing absenteeism. He calls a meeting of his direct reports to develop a creative solution to the problem. The problem is stated as "We have too much and ever-increasing absenteeism in our call centers." The framing question is simple, general, and without criteria: "How might we reduce absenteeism in our call centers?" Each person selects an image that represents the challenge from his or her perspective. Each of the images is shared using the basic Visual Explorer process.

As team members share their perceptions, a theme emerges about what their work in managing call centers means to them and what the work of call center operators means to them. These operators, not surprisingly, tend to find little meaning in their work beyond getting a paycheck. This leads to a reframing of the challenge: "In what ways might we help call center operators gain meaning from their work?" This is the reframed challenge statement that is taken into the idea generation phase of the creative problem-solving process—and eventually becomes part of the solution.

Visual Connections Worksheet

Challenge statement: ______________________________

____

____

____

Image 1: ______________________________

____

____

____

____

Connections: ______________________________

____

____

____

____

Image 2: ______________________________

____

____

____

____

Connections: ______________________________

____

____

____

____

Image 3: ______________________________

____

____

____

____

Connections: ______________________________

____

____

____

____

Image 4: ______________________________

____

____

____

____

Connections: ______________________________

____

____

____

____

Benefits of This Application

- Legitimizes intuitions and emotions
- Calls forth artistry
- Provokes new questions
- Generates alternatives
- Builds on ideas
- Encourages fun, playful, yet serious dialogue
- Taps into personal experiences and passions
- Draws careful attention to details and to the big picture
- Makes abstract conversations tangible
- Helps frame and illustrate thoughts so they can be shared
- Creates new metaphors
- Helps individuals and groups get unstuck
- Makes self-disclosure and vulnerability safe
- Produces tangible images that can be reused in paper and digital forms

A vision of the future is a guide to success, for an individual, a team, or an organization. Effective visioning is a whole-brain endeavor, requiring left-brain plus right-brain cognition, feelings plus reason, dry abstractions plus rich sensations, words plus images. Visual Explorer can be an aid to rounding out the right-brain part of visioning. It puts people in contact with their nonverbal selves, including intuitions and driving forces. Visual Explorer is especially useful at the initial stages of forming a vision, when diverse and heartfelt input is required. It is also a useful tool for preserving, crafting, and then communicating a vision, since the images can be reused in digital form.

Facilitation

Individual visioning facilitation follows the five-step Visual Explorer process. The framing questions and dialogues are individually oriented. For example, "How will the world look different as the result of my work? What will be my legacy? Where do I see myself in five years?" This type of facilitation applies to one-on-one coaching, as well as classes or programs in which the students or participants come from different organizations (for example, in individual leader development programs).

Collective visioning facilitation also follows the five-step Visual Explorer process. The framing questions and dialogues are now plural. For example, "How will the world look different as the result of our work? What will be our legacy? Where do we see ourselves in five years?" This kind of facilitation applies to intact teams of leaders from the same organization who seek a shared vision. This kind of collective visioning facilitation is closely related to organizational change and appreciative inquiry applications, and it is best applied organically within a larger change initiative, with the appropriate lead-in and follow-through when enacting the vision.

Example of This Application in Action

In this example of collective visioning, a leadership team in the health care industry used Visual Explorer to explore shared vision of its organization as it faced great challenges and changes. The team members participated in a standard Visual Explorer session per the instructions for dialogue, but with the framing questions focused on the future of the organization and the means of getting there: "Pick two images, one for each of these questions: What future do you envision for this organization? What has to change for us to get there?" After the session the team put these images into a slide show, overlaid with a few of the key ideas from the dialogue. The slide show became a vivid reminder for the team as they developed the vision over time, including more and more people. Some of the images were later used to communicate aspects of the vision throughout the organization.

An example of individual visioning is the case of Ellen Schall, Dean of New York University's Robert F. Wagner Graduate School of Public Service. In preparing for a recent graduation speech, Dean Schall chose an image that represented her vision of public service: the image of a potter at work. Some students in this graduating class had been admitted to the program based on an application that included an essay about their own visions of public service, represented by images they had selected ("What Do You See?" 2009). In Dean Schall's address, she shared the image she selected along with her story and vision. Here is an excerpt:

Related Applications

- Enabling dialogue
- Facing complex challenges
- Strategic leadership
- Change leadership
- Creating scenarios of the future
- Appreciative inquiry
- Individual coaching
- Team coaching
- Leadership development programs
- Youth and young adult education

Additional Resources for This Application

Cartwright & Baldwin. *Communicating Your Vision.*

Criswell & Cartwright. *Creating a Vision.*

NYU Wagner Congratulates the Class of 2009, and Celebrates Convocation at BAM.

Parker. *Creating Shared Vision.*

"What Do You See?"

Here is the image I chose: an image of a person—alas, not me—bringing a pot to life on a potter's wheel. I took a beginners' pottery class this past fall. I showed up every Monday night, from 6 to 9, much the way you showed up for a class. And it was *very* hard. I was the worst in the class, a fact clear to me and to everyone else. Yet I stayed and kept on trying. I knew there was learning in the trying, in sticking with what didn't come easily. I never actually cracked the code or became a potter. Yet at the end, I have these small little pieces of "pottery" in my house, and the odd thing is I display them. They are on the entry hall table and they make me smile when I walk in. They remind me to take myself seriously, but not too seriously, to stretch even in the face of initial resistance, mine or others, to find pleasure in small wins.

This [picture of a potter at work] captures in a simple visual image what I wish for each of you as you go forth. That you embrace the boldness of seeing yourself as artists, as creators and change makers, as people who bring passion and the fullness of your selves to the critically important challenges of public service. And that you have the discipline and energy and commitment to keep on going, even if you don't get it right the first time around, that you learn from what works—as well as what doesn't—and that you find joy in small things as well as big moves.

I believe more than ever in the need for artistry in the work of public service. We invited you to join us at Wagner to change the world. We offered you a varied set of tools and frameworks from which you can draw. But tools and frames alone don't do the trick. Public service is as much about art as science. When we bring artistry to public service, we bring passion, creativity, and the gift of seeing new possibilities. Holding a sense of ourselves as artists as we go about the work of public service helps us to stay bold and aim high.

CREATING SCENARIOS OF THE FUTURE

Scenarios of possible futures, deliberately explored, are used by organizations to navigate through complexity and uncertainty toward a preferred outcome. Creating such scenarios has become an increasingly common leadership tool. Creating scenarios of possible futures is a way to help with preparedness, strategic planning, and visioning (Schwartz, 1991). Scenario creation has an imaginative aspect in which people (leaders, managers, employees, citizens) picture alternative versions of the future using stories and images. An important feature of scenario creation is the dialogue that ensues when the scenarios are put into the middle of deep and probing conversations. Scenario creation involves serious play (Palus & Horth, 2002), such that the creation and exploration of the scenarios are playful and creative, yet grounded in serious inquiry. Visual Explorer supports these imaginative, dialogical, and playful aspects of future scenario creation.

Facilitation

A technique we call movie making is effective for creating and exploring future scenarios. The "movie" made is a wall-sized collage of images and words that tell an imaginative story about where an organization might be headed, or how certain challenges might worsen or resolve "once upon a time in a place not too far from here." Movie making facilitates assumption-testing dialogue about possible futures in a group faced with one or more complex challenges. These movies are fictions containing—and highlighting—important truths. Each movie explores its theme in an imaginative, fictive way, yet captures true ideas and valuable intuitions for further dialogue and testing.

Benefits of This Application

- Helps generate alternative futures for wiser planning
- Encourages fun, playful, yet serious dialogue
- Taps into personal experiences and passions
- Draws careful attention to details and to the big picture
- Makes abstract conversations tangible
- Helps frame and illustrate thoughts so they can be shared
- Surfaces individual and group assumptions
- Bridges different contexts and cultures
- Creates new metaphors
- Produces tangible images that can be reused in paper and digital forms
- Helps individuals and groups get unstuck

Additional Resources for This Application

de Geus. "Strategy and Learning."

Global Business Network: Ideas (Web site).

Mieszkowski. "Wild Cards."

Peterson. *Out of the Blue.*

Schwartz. *The Art of the Long View.*

van der Heijden. *Scenarios.*

Wack. "Scenarios, Shooting the Rapids."

When we work with a group, one or several themes in the challenge become apparent over the course of interviews and preliminary discussions. For a movie-making exercise we split the group into subgroups of four to eight people, and give each subgroup a theme, or have them select one for a movie. From all this it should be clear that movie making is ideally a collaborative, interdependent activity and in any case diagnostic of group dynamics.

Visual Explorer works well as the lead-in to the movie-making exercise, to determine the themes of the movies. Explore scenario-based framing questions in a Visual Explorer dialogue, such as "What are the big trends that will determine our future? What are we missing or overlooking or forgetting as we try to see the future? What might this organization look like in ten years? What would it look like to do our work digitally and virtually?"

From this initial Visual Explorer session, list and prioritize key themes that could influence the future of the organization. Use these to plot the movies. It's fun and instructive to add wild-card movie themes—for example, "What would happen if our senior team was run over by a bus?"

Materials

- long, wide paper for each group (about three meters [ten feet] long by one meter [three feet] high)
- scissors, tape, glue sticks
- magazines (a variety, lots of pages of images or graphics, familiar and unfamiliar)
- a set of Visual Explorer images
- markers, pens, paints, brushes, yarn, sticky notes (a variety)

Each subgroup combines words and images on a roll of white paper to create a movie. Use some words but mostly images and illustrations, in a narrative sequence over time, moving from left to right. You may reuse (cut up, glue, etc.) the Visual Explorer images from the previous exercise.

Your movie's plot has three parts. First: "Once upon a time, there was an organization or a thing like us . . . ." Second: "And then one day something happened—a catastrophe, an invention, a revolution, a new initiative! Or what?" Third: "This is how it all turns out for better or worse."

Show the movie to the group. Then use it as a springboard, as "something in the middle" for a dialogue exploring the theme. Make sure someone is writing it all down in detail (and video capture, photos, etc.), for further reuse and extraction of key lessons.

Designer's Tip

- If you want your participants to cut up their Visual Explorer images, you should make color photocopies of the images they selected earlier rather than cut up the originals.

- Don't skimp on the paper. Give your participants plenty of space to create.

- If you get stuck creating a plot, start arranging images on the roll of paper. Play with the visual ideas and the pieces of paper, and explain it all later.

- If you have conflict as you wrestle with the content of the movie, invent characters to represent the different ideas and put them *all* in the movie. Let the characters work out your conflict. Movies need not be about probable events. In fact, we find that the process works best when the group is instructed to build the plot around something "unexpected or even catastrophic." These days it is probable that something unexpected will happen.

- In debriefing the movie, ensure that the period from "And then one day . . ." is explored carefully so the movie doesn't simply jump from the stuck point to ". . . and they all lived happily ever after." Ask, "What practical, new processes and events occurred that contributed to our progress from being stuck to finding a meaningful outcome?"

When making movies within organizations, there are certain situations that may develop and you should keep them in mind as you guide participants. For the session, participants should finish with convergence, harvest the best ideas, and plan next steps and responsibilities.

The Hesitant Group: Before the process begins, people might be concerned that movie making will be too touchy-feely. These concerns almost always fade during the dialogue, as real business issues get explored in depth and detail. In fact, increased "touch and feel" about complex issues is a key objective of the exercise. The focus on real business challenges while harvesting valuable insights is a key validation of the exercise.

Opposition in the Group: Having something in the middle of the group—the movies—allows opposing ideas a common focus. The dialogue that follows the making of the movies is the real point of this exercise. If groups experience conflict as they make the movie, suggest they craft their conflict into opposing characters, put them into the movie, and see how it comes out.

Analytical Overdrive: When groups start designing movies, their conversation often begins in abstractions and analysis. You can facilitate the imaging process by encouraging them to go up to the wall and physically start sketching out the ideas. At the wall, people usually become more intuitive, imaginative, and playful.

Valuable Metaphors: Metaphors created in these movies usually contain insights about the state of the organization, where it's headed, and the means to get there. Your group can take away these metaphors and use them to craft and communicate its mission, vision, and values.

Rough Takes: Keep in mind that movies are more like unpolished drafts than finished scripts. They tend to be nonlinear and less integrated than a traditional story. These qualities are actually helpful to the ensuing dialogue since they invite revision and further what-ifs.

A vice president of software development used movie making with a large, diverse group of people to explore a critical issue facing her division. All the attendees at the meeting were leaders of functional groups. Some were her direct reports; the rest were supervisors who reported to her direct reports. She created two groups of four each. She covered the walls with white rolls of paper, and provided Visual Explorer images, pages of images from magazines, markers, ribbon, glue sticks, stickers, string, and other craft materials. She instructed them to work fast and to make their movies "as provocative as hell." And they did!

One group created a movie that went something like this: Once upon a time there were four friends who worked at a computer software company which looked like . . . this. Then one day (December 31, 1999, to be exact), they committed the perfect crime. They broke into the company directory and payroll system and changed all the employee titles and salaries. Bosses became subordinates, and subordinates became bosses. This created an interesting series of situations, in which people saw issues and problems from totally different perspectives and were better able to solve problems because of these new perspectives. The closing frame is the words *Live the Dream*.

This movie stimulated a powerful dialogue on these points:

- the need to see issues from more than one perspective

- the importance of acknowledging the perspective of corporate management

- the importance of acknowledging our clients' needs

- the importance of acknowledging our staff's needs and balancing them with what our clients need

- the need to "shield" our clients from our internal problems and issues

- the need to help staff see their clients' perspectives

- the need to improve communication of needs and expectations

Benefits of This Application

- Legitimizes intuition
- Calls forth artistry
- Provokes new questions
- Generates alternatives
- Builds on ideas
- Builds direction, alignment, and commitment
- Encourages fun, playful, yet serious dialogue
- Taps into personal experiences and passions
- Draws careful attention to details and to the big picture
- Bridges different context and cultures
- Creates new metaphors
- Makes conversations both artful and analytical
- Helps individuals and groups get unstuck
- Produces tangible images that can be reused in paper and digital forms
- Surfaces, engages, and transcends emotional undercurrents

Appreciative inquiry is an organization development approach based on shared inquiry. Its methods frame questions appreciatively, in ways that evoke positive stories and images of the past, present, and future. Appreciative inquiry studies and explores what gives life to human systems when they function at their best (see Cooperrider & Whitney, 2006). Visual Explorer supports appreciative inquiry by providing a scaffold for positive storytelling, imagination, and dialogue. Since the images can be saved and reused, sequenced, collaged, etc., Visual Explorer is especially good for building positive stories over time, as the journey of appreciative inquiry unfolds. Visual Explorer is a natural fit with the appreciative inquiry stages of discovery and dreaming.

Facilitation

In using Visual Explorer to facilitate steps in appreciative inquiry, follow the five basic Visual Explorer process steps, and use the dialogue application instructions to deepen and extend the ensuing conversations. The planners and facilitators of the Visual Explorer session must be familiar with appreciative inquiry as a philosophy and set of practices. To get started with appreciative inquiry, see Cooperrider and Whitney (2006).

Example of This Application in Action

This example of Visual Explorer applied to appreciative inquiry comes from our colleague Bruce Flye, Director of Planning and Partnerships at the Brody School of Medicine at East Carolina University. Bruce has developed his drawing and design skills to enhance his facilitations with graphics, which often become tokens, symbols, reminders, or simply takeaways for his participants (see Figure 11, page 70, for example).

I recently worked with an information technology services group in thinking through the changes emerging in their work. The design approach was framed around appreciative inquiry in the specific form of the S.O.A.R. model (for Strengths, Opportunities, Aspirations, and Results; Stavros, Cooperrider, & Kelley, 2003). The *A* is for *aspirations*, and to work with that, we used Visual Explorer.

The group had worked through an extensive discovery phase over the summer, and prior to this session a few came together and synthesized their findings into strengths and opportunities. Working from those, we articulated the group's purpose. The group members were then asked to think for a few minutes and create a mental image about what life would be like if they were fluidly deploying those strengths and opportunities and serving that purpose.

Around the room we had scattered the Visual Explorer postcards. We invited everyone to select one that best represented his or her mental image. They then worked in pairs to share their selections and thoughts, and subsequently the whole group worked with a brainstorming process to describe its shared aspirations.

Five aspirations emerged. Once they were on the wall, the group was asked if one of its selected Visual Explorer cards seemed to describe each aspiration. The answer was that some aspirations merited more than one image. They were then asked if there was a single image that

Related Applications

- Enabling dialogue
- Facing complex challenges
- Strategic leadership
- Change leadership
- Creative problem solving
- Visioning
- Creating scenarios of the future
- Leadership development programs
- Youth and young adult education
- Retreats and off-site meetings

Additional Resources for This Application

Appreciative Inquiry Commons (Web site).

Bruce Flye.

Cooperrider & Whitney. "Appreciative Inquiry."

Selvin. "Performing Knowledge Art."

Selvin et al. "Compendium."

Stavros, Cooperrider, & Kelley. *Strategic Inquiry → Appreciative Intent.*

seemed to represent the collection of aspirations, and they chose two: a picture of puzzle pieces as a description of where they were then, and a photo of Stonehenge to represent the firmness and completeness of their future (Figure 11).

Figure 11. The image of a puzzle becomes a group's key metaphor for its shared aspirations.
Source: Bruce Flye. Used with permission.

Benefits of This Application

- Supports key leadership perspectives and abilities such as vision, perspective taking, imagination, and creativity
- Supports presence in expression and communication
- Helps the client navigate turbulence and complexity
- Builds positive client-coach relationships
- Supports positive development and whole-person functioning
- Supports the coaches themselves
- Supports brief coaching
- Engages intuition and emotion
- Provokes new questions
- Generates alternatives
- Encourages fun, playful, yet serious dialogue

Visual Explorer is an engaging, interactive tool for meaning-making that supports a variety of individual coaching processes, including one-on-one leadership coaching, impromptu creative conversations, and self-coaching. Visual Explorer thus applied is a form of artful coaching—the application of abilities, mental models, media, and methods from the arts to the coaching of managers, professionals, and leaders (Palus, 2006).

Visual Explorer typically creates deeper dialogue and better insights in coaching situations. Once again, we find that images are a powerful mediating device in conversations. The provocative and interesting images, and the metaphors and memories they suggest, help people open up to the nonverbal side of what they know, including subconscious insights and wordless emotions and intuitions. Along with this opening, Visual Explorer provides a bridge, between coachee and coach, across differences in personal, demographic, and cultural worldviews (Ernst & Yip, 2009; Rosinski, 2003). The focal images provide a common ground visible to both coach and coachee. Handling the images, arranging them, and "playing" with them are part of the power. This physical, tactile interplay creates moving bodies rather than talking heads. Many people find it relaxing to do something with their hands. Tacit knowledge flows into body language. Did we mention that this can be lots of fun? The fact that the images are literally in the middle of the conversation changes the interpersonal dynamic from "eye to eye" to "let's explore this something-in-the-middle." Imagination easily enters this space.

Facilitation

Visual Explorer works well in coaching contexts ranging from formal to impromptu. The card-sized

- Enabling dialogue
- Facing complex challenges
- Strategic leadership
- Change leadership
- Creative problem solving
- Visioning
- Creating scenarios of the future
- Appreciative inquiry
- Individual coaching
- Leadership development programs
- Feedback and performance appraisals

versions of Visual Explorer work best since they are portable and easily spread out on a desktop or thumbed through by hand. Typically, Visual Explorer is used with four types of coaching-related framing questions: (1) big picture or integration, (2) future aspirations, (3) unspoken insights and emotions and difficult subjects to verbalize, and (4) presence (right now). Visual Explorer is usually used toward the middle or end of a coaching session and used to sum up, fully express, and integrate what came before. Often coaches like to "warm up" with the coachee before using Visual Explorer and gauge readiness to do a possibly unfamiliar exercise involving a deeper level of candor. Coaches often keep a Visual Explorer deck handy for moments of opportunity for impromptu coaching—for example, at lunch, in the lobby, or at the airport.

Once again, the five basic steps of the Visual Explorer process generally apply, and they can be modified to the particular coaching context. The key is to tailor the framing questions to the needs of the coachee. Big picture and integration framing questions include "How does the feedback data we've discussed all fit together; what are the key insights for you? What are the key influences and experiences in your life that have shaped you as a leader?" Future aspiration framing questions include "How will you put what you learned into practice? What is the most important thing you want for yourself? Your family? Your organization? What will be your legacy?" Framing questions that reach for unspoken or difficult insights include "What is your best quality as a person? As a leader? What's getting in your way? What's still missing from this discussion we've been having? What else is going on? What are the deepest desires of your heart?" Presence questions invoke the elusive territory of "right now," a wonderful move for all of us who tend to live in the past and future. These questions include "Where are you right now? How do you feel, now? What's going on for you right now?" Presence questions can be valuable at the beginning of a session when the coach and coachee already know each other, so that what the coachee is "carrying" at that moment can be both surfaced as valuable data and "left at the door" after recognition.

Example of This Application in Action

The following example is from the blog of TZiPi Radonsky (2007), a CCL leadership coach adept at connecting with people using Visual Explorer images.

Who would imagine that the images would evoke such emotional responses that they would bring tears, conversations never dreamed in a coaching session, and clarity and validation of goals? I usually use the Visual Explorer cards at the end of the session, as I feel that if people connect an image with their goals, it might mean more to them than the words themselves. I am always hoping for an intention to appear—a symbol that would reflect an emotion, a private thought, or a connection to core values that is attached to the outcome, in contrast to a goal that is more in the physical world of doing.

Alice (not her real name) was a member of a leadership training program for women. The role she played was highly visible in a male-dominated profession, and she wanted "to play hardball with the boys." Yes, this is a direct quote. On paper she was enthusiastic and energetic about life. In person she appeared tired and pensive. By the end of the session, she admitted that her Catholic upbringing had led her to believe

Additional Resources for This Application

Ernst & Chrobot-Mason. *Boundary Spanning Leadership.*

Ernst & Yip. *Boundary Spanning Leadership.*

Goldsmith & Lyons. *Coaching for Leadership.*

Hart & Miller. *Using Your Executive Coach.*

Lakoff & Johnson. *Metaphors We Live By.*

Morgan. *Images of Organizations.*

Morgan, Harkins, & Goldsmith. *The Art and Practice of Leadership Coaching.*

Palus. (2004). *Artful Coaching.*

Palus. (2006). "Artful Coaching."

Radonsky. "The Mystery of the Cards."

Rosinski. *Coaching across Cultures.*

Ting & Scisco. *The CCL Handbook of Coaching.*

and act that women needed to defer to men or anyone who wielded power. There was some cognitive dissonance in relation to her ambitious nature. I asked her to pick a card: "Where are you right now?" To her surprise, she picked an image of five boys and one girl in a semicircle with their backs to the camera. After thinking about that image, Alice said, "I guess I already am playing hardball with the boys, and maybe I need to act with that attitude." She later e-mailed to say that she had gone to speak with her boss, a man, and had asked for more challenges, which he offered to her.

Benefits of This Application

- Encourages fun, playful, yet serious dialogue
- Builds direction, alignment, and commitment
- Clarifies and communicates mission, vision, and values
- Draws attention to details and to the big picture
- Surfaces individual and group assumptions
- Provokes new questions
- Generates alternatives
- Builds on ideas
- Bridges different contexts and cultures
- Creates new metaphors
- Encourages sharing of perspectives in a way that leads to the construction of new perspectives
- Makes self-disclosure and vulnerability safe
- Taps into personal experiences and passions
- Helps individuals and groups get unstuck

Visual Explorer has broad applications for leading teams, team coaching, and team building. It is useful for facilitating reflection and effective dialogue at any stage of team development and in a wide variety of team-based processes, such as feedback, brainstorming, creative problem solving, strategy making, visioning, and appreciative inquiry.

Facilitation

The five steps of the basic Visual Explorer instructions apply to team coaching, though with intact teams more improvisation is possible. The framing questions for the Visual Explorer session should always be adapted to what the team needs at that particular moment. Team needs and the best framing questions can be understood in terms of the Drexler Sibbet Team Performance Model (Drexler, Sibbet, & Forrester, 2003). Here are the seven phases of that model, with seven framing questions:

1. Orientation: "Why am I here?"
2. Trust building: "Who are you?"
3. Goal clarification: "What are we doing?"
4. Commitment: "How will we do it?"
5. Implementation: "Who does what, when, where?"
6. High performance: "How does it feel?"
7. Renewal: "Why continue?"

In addition, there are great framing questions that run across all of these phases: "What's it like for me to work on this team? How are we doing (am I doing) right now? What are we like at our best? What are we not paying (enough) attention to? What is missing? What do we (I) dream of?"

Related Applications

- Enabling dialogue
- Facing complex challenges
- Strategic leadership
- Change leadership
- Creative problem solving
- Visioning
- Creating scenarios of the future
- Appreciative inquiry
- Individual coaching
- Leadership development programs
- Feedback and performance appraisals
- Youth and young adult education
- Retreats and off-site meetings

Example of This Application in Action

ACME (made-up name), a large insurance and financial company, has been using Visual Explorer as a tool for team building within work groups. Katie Davis, a consultant and trainer with the company, has found that visual images are a great tool for building trust and alignment when teams come together to resolve problems and tackle opportunities. "It's not unusual for individuals in a work group—even those that have been together for a long time—to be ill at ease with each other," Davis says. "Using photos and images brings safety. You're not talking about yourself. Instead, you're talking about a picture. That's safer for folks and inspires confidence." Photos can also level the playing field and give everyone a voice, she points out. "When you have a discussion in a group, typically there are the people who jump in and dominate, and there are the people you never hear from. Using this format creates the expectation that everyone will share."

Davis says that images are also useful to help teams define and develop a shared understanding of a concept. She likes to ask members of a group to select a picture that represents a quality of their dream team—transferring the characteristics that people describe on paper and then hanging the papers on the wall. "We then distill those and get down to the five or six core values that are held by the team," she says. "It's also a powerful tool to help define what a word such as *honesty* means and to build a common understanding."

Davis points to one work group that used images to define what *accountability* meant to them. Participants prepared a summary of their session, as Davis asked each team to do, and came back to the information time and time again as they addressed real-world challenges. They began to call each other on not living up to the principles they had established as a team and to use their shared experience to resolve business issues. They also agreed to share accountability and take on more work so that the company could save money by not filling an open position in their work group. "Nothing I could've done with them could have gotten them to that point without the image tool," she says.

Additional Resources for This Application

Britton. *Effective Group Coaching.*

Drexler, Sibbet, & Forrester. *The Team Performance Model.*

Ernst & Chrobot-Mason. *Boundary Spanning Leadership.*

Ernst & Yip. *Boundary Spanning Leadership.*

Horth & Palus. "Using Visuals to Build Teams."

Palus & Drath. *Putting Something in the Middle.*

Palus & Horth. *The Leader's Edge.*

Rosinski. *Coaching across Cultures.*

Sibbet. *Visual Meetings.*

Benefits of This Application

- Encourages fun, playful, yet serious dialogue
- Builds direction, alignment, and commitment
- Taps into personal experiences and passions
- Helps frame and illustrate thoughts so they can be shared
- Surfaces individual and group assumptions
- Bridges different contexts and cultures
- Creates new metaphors
- Makes conversations both artful and analytical
- Makes self-disclosure and vulnerability safe
- Produces tangible images that can be reused in paper and digital forms
- Enables an experience of skilled conversation or dialogue
- Surfaces ideas and new perspectives

Visual Explorer has been widely used in leadership development programs, with participants ranging from senior executives to youth leaders to members of self-help groups. In leadership development programs Visual Explorer is often used in capturing expectations for the program, talking about definitions of leadership, exploring challenges in the program, and goal setting.

Facilitation

The five basic steps of a Visual Explorer process also apply in a leadership development program. Depending on the design of the program, many applications of Visual Explorer can be adapted, including dialogue, appreciative inquiry, and strategic leadership. Visual Explorer can focus on individual leaders (goals and vision, for example) or on collective leadership (shared strategy and practices within a single organization, for example).

A Visual Explorer session can be designed to elicit the participant's experiences and contexts of leadership, with framing questions such as these: "How is leadership done where you work? What does it typically look like in action? What is the leadership culture of your workplace?"

Visual Explorer is useful in establishing a creative and fun climate within programs. The selected images can be used multiple times during and after the program to remember and reimagine the meanings attached to the images, as we see in the following example.

Example of This Application in Action

We worked with a services company in designing a Visual Explorer session for participants to share leadership values, vision, and best practices during an advanced leadership lab. The three framing questions were as follows:

1. What is it like to lead at this company today?

2. What do you hope leadership at this company will look like one to two years from now?

3. What is something specific you are doing or seeing now that could be used effectively by others to meet the leadership needs of the next one to two years? In other words, what is one forward-looking best practice of leadership at this company?

Each participant picked one image for each question, wrote notes in a reflections worksheet, and then circled up in groups of four or five for dialogues. We enforced no talking during browsing while jazz played in the background.

From the ensuing dialogue, participants received great insight from each other and together produced wholly new insights. The facilitator created a "visual verbal slideshow" combining the chosen images with the words participants wrote on a worksheet (see Figures 12, 13, and 14). This slideshow, completed overnight, was shown the next day, resulting in even more engagement around key insights. Excerpts from the slideshow are shown on page 80.

Related Applications

- Enabling dialogue
- Facing complex challenges
- Strategic leadership
- Change leadership
- Visioning
- Creating scenarios of the future
- Appreciative inquiry
- Feedback and performance appraisals
- Youth and young adult education
- Retreats and off-site meetings

Additional Resources for This Application

Drath & Palus. *Making Common Sense.*

Ernst & Chrobot-Mason. *Boundary Spanning Leadership.*

Palus & Drath. *Evolving Leaders.*

Palus & Drath. *Putting Something in the Middle.*

Pasmore & Lafferty. *Developing a Leadership Strategy.*

Figures 12, 13, and 14. A slideshow composed of images and insights engages a team in defining how it sees leadership. *Photographs provided by Getty Images, Inc., ©2004. All Rights Reserved.*

Visual Explorer can be used to create more open, meaningful, and candid (and therefore more effective) conversations about performance appraisals or almost any type of feedback. Performance conversations run the risk of being overly impersonal, guarded, and analytical. Visual Explorer helps people open up in feedback and appraisal situations where they might otherwise shut down.

Facilitation

Visual Explorer works well in feedback situations ranging from formal performance appraisals to impromptu conversations. The card-sized versions of Visual Explorer work best since they are portable and easily spread out on a desktop or thumbed through by hand. Visual Explorer is typically used with four types of feedback and performance-oriented framing questions: (1) strengths and weaknesses, (2) integration of data, (3) big picture, and (4) future aspirations. Visual Explorer is usually used toward the middle or end of a feedback or appraisal session and used to sum up, fully express, and integrate what came before.

Once again, the five basic steps of the Visual Explorer process generally apply, and they can be modified to fit the particular feedback context. The key is to tailor the framing questions to the needs of the situation. A framing question for strengths and weaknesses is "Pick one card that shows your strengths as a manager and one card that shows your weaknesses." Integrative framing questions include "How would you sum up all the feedback data you've been looking at today? What's the main insight you will take away?" Big picture framing questions include "What defines you as a leader? How would you sum up your contribution to this

Benefits of This Application

- Creates fresh insights
- Generates alternatives
- Engages intuitions and emotions
- Promotes openness and honesty
- Provokes new questions
- Encourages fun, playful, yet serious dialogue
- Taps into personal experiences and passions
- Makes tangible otherwise abstract conversations
- Builds direction, alignment, and commitment
- Helps frame and illustrate thoughts so they can be shared
- Bridges different contexts and cultures
- Creates new metaphors

- Enabling dialogue
- Facing complex challenges
- Strategic leadership
- Change leadership
- Creative problem solving
- Visioning
- Appreciative inquiry
- Individual coaching

organization?" Future aspiration framing questions include "What do want in your career? What is your biggest aspiration? What do you want your legacy to be?"

Example of This Application in Action

Consider the example of Chris Barnes, the director of the Orion corporate research center for creating advanced polymers used in consumer products (all names are disguised). Orion is becoming more of a learning organization, and Chris's new role emphasizes participative leadership and shared learning. It was time for performance appraisals. Chris sat down with his direct report Ki-Hun, a senior research scientist. Ki-Hun is a native of Korea and one of the many professionals at the research center for whom English is a second language. To prepare for the meeting, both Chris and Ki-Hun reviewed Ki-Hun's objectives and accomplishments for the year, part of a management-by-objectives system. In spite of Ki-Hun's many achievements for the year, neither of them was looking forward to the session. In the past, performance appraisals had been stilted and awkward, and had glossed over both the high points and the low points. Language and culture differences always seemed to add to the discomfort.

So Chris tried a different approach this time. He said, "Ki-Hun, I feel that there are some important things about your work that we aren't getting at with this list of objectives. I have a conversation tool for us to try called Visual Explorer. What do you think? How about if we each pick several pictures that represent the positive things about your work this year, and likewise several more that get at your frustrations this year. Then we'll share the pictures we've picked and talk about them." Chris shared the Visual Explorer card deck and spread out the images on the desktop. The ensuing conversation was free-flowing and surprisingly candid. They laughed a lot, as when Ki-Hun admitted that he felt "like this goat in the picture" when his project tied up the electron microscope for a month without anything to show for it. Both Chris and Ki-Hun walked away from the performance appraisal feeling satisfied. Chris had been able to say some tough things to Ki-Hun, while also expressing in a vivid way his perception that Ki-Hun was potentially a star performer. And Ki-Hun remembered for a long time the picture Chris chose of an eagle in flight, and what it means to be a star performer who is sometimes isolated from his peers.

Additional Resources for This Application

Buron & McDonald-Mann. *Giving Feedback to Subordinates.*

Fleenor, Taylor, & Chappelow. *Leveraging the Impact of 360-Degree Feedback.*

Hoppe. *Active Listening.*

Hughes & Beatty. *Becoming a Strategic Leader.*

Palus & Horth. *The Leader's Edge.*

Tornow, London, & the Center for Creative Leadership. *Maximizing the Value of 360-Degree Feedback.*

Weitzel. *Feedback That Works.*

Benefits of This Application

- Elicits underlying metaphors and stories

- Enables communication of emotions, intuitions, and tacit knowledge that would otherwise be unspoken and undiscovered

- Taps into personal experiences and passions

- Helps frame and illustrate thoughts so they can be shared

- Makes the invisible visible and the unconscious conscious

- Bridges different contexts and cultures

- Encourages fun, playful, yet serious dialogue

- Makes self-disclosure and vulnerability safe

- Produces tangible images that can be reused in paper and digital forms

Visual Explorer lends itself well to ethnography and cultural anthropology, ranging from market research, generational studies, and program evaluations to basic research. Formats include focus groups, interviews, online surveys, and shared browsers. Why Visual Explorer? People know more than they can put into words. Sometimes simple verbal transactions obscure what we most want to know. Knowledge, including self-knowledge and cultural knowledge, is vastly unconscious, intuitive, emotional, visceral, symbolic, and imaginal. For this kind of knowledge, imagery, metaphor, and stories provide a vibrant language. Visual Explorer is a way of enriching these research conversations, while more fully engaging the audience's interest, and thus producing more valid and more useful knowledge.

Facilitation

The key to using Visual Explorer for ethnographic research is to engage participants in a creative conversation among themselves, and with the researchers, and to document the conversation. For example, focus groups can be created around any topic of interest to the researchers and the target population. Allow the group to individually and collectively select as many images as they want in response to the framing question. You might also ask them to pick a set of images which they think contradict the question or answer it in the negative. Record their selections along with their discussion. Then ask them to group the set of selected images and discuss the grouping. Ask for a key image that captures each group. Repeat the process with a sufficient number of groups to look for consistency and variability in the responses. Look for the rare or weak signals as well as the strong ones. Researchers analyze for themes and triangulate with other relevant data for convergent insights.

Example of This Application in Action

Neelus, an innovation consulting company based in Argentina, uses Visual Explorer with its clients in its core methodologies of insight, ideation, and prototyping. Neelus undertook a bold project to understand the future of the marketplace. As part of this, the company sought to understand the worldviews and preferences of Generation Y (aged 17 to 25) as they might evolve across the next decade. These young people face great social uncertainties and challenges, and are the first generation to fully experience a globalized economy. Clients had come to Neelus with their problems in understanding this generation and in dealing with differences from prior generations. Neelus and its clients had several key questions:

1. How might we segment the new so-called Generation Y in Argentina?

2. How do those young people relate to the future? What are their dreams for the future?

3. How does Generation Y understand relationships between themselves and significant others?

4. What are their expectations for jobs and careers? What should companies do to gain acceptance and raise motivation among those young people?

5. What are the implications for their behaviors and attitudes toward brands?

Related Applications

- Visioning
- Creating scenarios of the future
- Appreciative inquiry
- Evaluation

Additional Resources for This Application

Ernst & Chrobot-Mason. *Boundary Spanning Leadership*.

Ernst & Yip. *Boundary Spanning Leadership*.

Pink. "Metaphor Marketing."

Rosinski. *Coaching across Cultures*.

Selvin. "Performing Knowledge Art."

Selvin et al. "Compendium."

Suri & Howard. "Going Deeper, Seeing Further."

Zaltman. *How Customers Think*.

Zaltman & Coulter. "Seeing the Voice of the Customer."

Zaltman & Zaltman. *Marketing Metaphoria*.

Neelus addressed these questions through three linked research methodologies:

1. Ethnographic observation: visiting universities, public places, jobs, etc., in order to observe how they move, what they do, what they use, etc.

2. Quantitative surveys: responding to specific questions about preferences etc., on numerical scales

3. Metaphoric exploration: using Visual Explorer, collage, and dialogue

Neelus understood that what people say and even what they do are not sufficient for the deeper kinds of understanding they sought—that it is critical to understand what people mean, underneath their actions and words. According to Alvaro Rolon, Neelus cofounder, they used Visual Explorer to understand "what they think and feel in a subtler way, about what they expect, what their dreams are, and their fantasies."

Neelus sampled a total of 63 young people, aged 17 to 25, some studying at university and some working. Fourteen small groups were formed, each focusing its deeper exploration on one of four areas: life, work, relationships, and leisure/fun. Because the key questions are mainly future oriented (expectations, dreams, careers), each group had a framing question of the form "What will life [or work, relationships, or leisure] be like in the year 2020?"

Each group was led by a psychologist trained in the process. First, each person chose an image in response to the group's framing question (and it worked well to add the suggestion ". . . or let the image choose you"). Each person then filled out a worksheet about his or her perceptions and interpretations of the image in light of the question. Each person then spoke to the group about his or her image.

Next, each group built a collage of images to represent its collective answer to the framing questions and had a creative conversation with the collage and its meanings in the middle.

The final step in the two-hour process was a dialogue about metaphors. The group was asked, "What metaphor would you use in response to the question, For me living [working, etc.] in the future is like . . . what?" According to Alvaro, "The conversation around the metaphors is when the subtle content came out. People crying . . . that's when the deep stuff came up, like therapy." Finally, Neelus convened an interdisciplinary group of experts to put all the results on the table and interpret themes (see Figure 15 for an example).

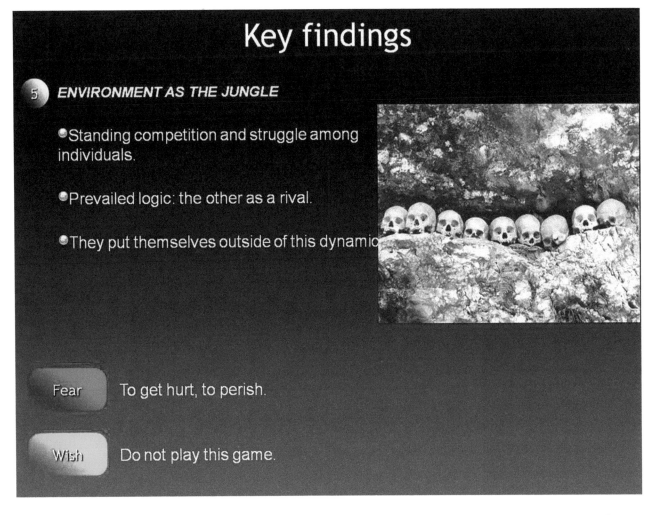

Figure 15. Neelus used Visual Explorer to probe the worldviews and preferences of young people in Argentina. *Photographs provided by Getty Images, Inc., ©2004. All Rights Reserved.*

Benefits of This Application

- Taps into personal experiences and passions
- Surfaces, engages, and transcends emotional undercurrents
- Helps frame and illustrate thoughts so they can be shared
- Surfaces individual and group assumptions
- Makes self-disclosure and vulnerability safe
- Encourages understanding of multidimensional concepts
- Bridges different context and cultures

Images can be used in a wide variety of ways to collect and communicate evaluation data (Hoole & Hannum, 2008). Images have great power to surface insights and to cross interpersonal, language, and cultural boundaries. When an evaluation process has a need to uncover assumptions and create meaning, a mediated dialogue approach using images may be a fruitful process. The use of images in evaluation dialogues can enhance data collection, collective sense-making by a group, and communicating experiences and participants' realities to a broad set of stakeholders.

Other researchers within the visual sociology, ethnography, and anthropology fields have found photography a valuable means of qualitative research (Brace-Govan, 2007; Schwartz, 1989). According to Weade and Ernst (2001, p. 133),

> They [metaphors] take us beyond the particular, the literal, and the moment-to-moment details of everyday experience. . . . Language, then, provides ways of assigning meaning to what we encounter visually, and it enables us to extend or enhance our interpretations of what we see.

Facilitation

There are many ways to use images as part of an evaluation process:

- Interviews: Ask an individual to select or bring an image that is representative of his or her experience or based upon a specific evaluation question. Look at pre- and postprogram images to understand change over time.

- Focus groups: Allow participants to select or bring one or more images to discuss with additional perspectives from group members. This helps to facilitate sense-making of the data, experiences, and outcomes.

- Creating a story board: An individual or group can use images (pictures, drawings) to tell the story of their journey over time (past, present, future scenes).

- Creating a collage: An individual or group collage can help to uncover connections and patterns not apparent through group discussions.

- Needs assessment: At the individual or group level, use images to understand the current situation, needs, and desired future state.

- Appreciative inquiry: Help people to express (using images, words, and stories) the positives or strengths within their communities (or cohorts, teams, etc.).

- Vision setting: Help a group to create a positive vision of the future.

The five steps of the basic Visual Explorer process generally apply. It is important to slow down and use the images for focused attention, reflection, and dialogue (rather than something merely light and fun).

As part of the framing of the session, it can be helpful to have an introductory portion that connects the individual or participant with the "object" or "evaluand" that will be the focus. For example, if the purpose is to evaluate the program implementation, it might be beneficial to review the program process from beginning to end, to prime recollection. Selecting the right framing question(s) is important. The process of evaluation has already done most of the framing: What questions are you asking in your evaluative study? What are you trying to learn? Reframe your research questions in ways the individual and/or group can answer them from their direct experience. For example: "Think about the positive things that have happened in your school as a result of your participation in the program. Select an image that represents the changes in your school as a result of your development as a leader."

The extend phase of the Visual Explorer process is key for evaluation. Combining images with other evaluation data creates a comprehensive

- Visioning
- Creating scenarios of the future
- Appreciative inquiry
- Ethnography and market research

picture of evaluation results. The evocative nature of images can serve as a powerful mechanism for communicating findings that can speak to different stakeholder groups in a way that may convey the evaluation results meaningfully and accurately. Images and metaphors can prompt deep reflection on the personal experience and illustrate the impact of a program to stakeholders in a way that is more accessible than graphs and tables. In order for evaluations to be useful, stakeholders must engage in the process of evaluation and understand the results of (and implications of) the evaluation.

These stakeholders include the following:

- The participants themselves: Seeing their individual and group experiences communicated provides a sense of empowerment and continues to deepen the relationship between participants and the evaluator and program staff.

- Staff: Seeing the images and explanations can help them gain new perspectives on their work.

- Funders: Images go beyond graphs and numbers to provide a window into the multiple realities constructed by individuals, groups, and communities.

- Communities: The adage "a picture is worth a thousand words" can be realized when using images to convey the value of a program to the public. When it was the community itself that participated in an initiative, providing the images creates a powerful sense of ownership.

Images and the metaphors provided during the evaluation can be put into a PowerPoint presentation, report, scrapbook, wall collage, or other medium for presentation. Combining a graph or table with a corresponding image helps to provide multiple perspectives and triangulation of the data. It can also help to spark meaningful dialogue with the stakeholder group.

Additional Resources for This Application

Brace-Govan. "Participant Photography in Visual Ethnography."

Drath & Palus. *Making Common Sense.*

Palus & Drath. *Putting Something in the Middle.*

Schwartz. "Visual Ethnography."

Selvin. "Performing Knowledge Art."

Ullman. *Appreciating Dreams.*

Weade & Ernst. "Pictures of Life in Classrooms, and the Search for Metaphors to Frame Them."

Example of This Application in Action

XYZ Company is a global aerospace products company with over $1B in revenue (all names are disguised). XYZ has for years been committed to leadership development at all levels of the organization. As part of this the company is intensely interested in evaluating the outcomes of leadership development, as well as identifying areas needing further development. We did a survey looking at the leadership culture (McGuire & Rhodes, 2009) with a cross section of managers, several cohorts of the same flagship XYZ leadership development program. The survey identified these two items as among the lowest scores:

- People do not talk about their mistakes.

- Leaders are conservative in their approach to risk and change.

The CEO asked us to take a closer look. What was going on? We convened a number of focus groups of the managers involved in the survey, and asked them to have a conversation with us, and with each other, about where these low scores came from, what they meant, and how to improve them. These conversations were set up in a safe way, without others from XYZ there, and with the promise of anonymity.

Each focus group did a Visual Explorer session as the key data-gathering and sense-making technique (Drath & Palus, 1994). We followed the five basic steps of the Visual Explorer process, using the following two framing questions, along with worksheets for written personal reflections:

1. Are these [the survey items mentioned above] accurate statements? Why?

2. What would improvement look like regarding risks and mistakes?

Each person picked one Visual Explorer card for each question and then shared his or her cards and reflections in an open and honest dialogue. In the role of facilitator-researchers, we took notes and asked follow-on questions during the dialogue. As part of the extension of the Visual Explorer session back into the work of the organization, we prepared a written report of the dialogue, as well as a slideshow combining the images and key insights.

Visual Explorer is very effective with children and young adults. Educators have successfully used the tool with students from preschool (using selected images) through university age, on every continent. Visual Explorer is a visual, interactive tool for engaging with an endless variety of topics and concepts, and for teaching the basics of dialogue. It supports the integration of different learning styles, invites quiet voices into the classroom conversation, and fosters exchanges across different perspectives, cultures, and languages. It provides a channel for intuitions, emotions, and imagination, and its combination of "serious" and "play" resonates with younger audiences.

Facilitation

Young people can typically engage in any of the applications in this facilitator's guide in age-appropriate ways. Educators sometimes use subsets of the Visual Explorer images related to the specific topics under discussion. The standard edition of Visual Explorer images is well suited to this application, but teachers who want a specially designed Visual Explorer tool for the classroom can examine the educator's edition published by About Learning. A description of that edition is available at the About Learning Web site (see URL in this guide's References and Resources section).

Example of This Application in Action

Here is a fascinating case of using Visual Explorer to conduct preprogram interviews and work with participants in youth programs. Lisa Markwick at the University of Auckland Business School describes her work at Excelerator, the New Zealand Leadership Institute:

Benefits of This Application

- Makes connections across multiple disciplines
- Uses images as building blocks to achieve higher levels of understanding and dialogue
- Helps with seeing patterns and relationships among ideas
- Engages diverse backgrounds, cultures, viewpoints, and opinions
- Teaches and reinforces the concepts and behaviors of dialogue and shared inquiry

We run (and research) a variety of different leadership development programmes, with our most established being our 18-month development programmes. These are targeted towards a number of different contexts, including the future leaders programme, community programmes (defining community as a geographic region), corporate programmes, and senior executive (cross-sectorial) programmes. We have plenty of opportunity to engage participants and others in creative and strategic practices and processes where we have found Visual Explorer to be a very powerful starter cue.

Let me tell you an example. I was in Dargaville meeting a group of prospective participants for a youth leadership programme. Dargaville is a rather depressed town about three hours north of Auckland, and the main centre of the Kaipara district where we had just been running an 18-month community leadership programme. I asked this group of six young people to each choose two pictures, one to represent a possibility for the future of Kaipara, and the other to demonstrate their commitment to participation in making it so. One of the young women chose a picture of a whole lot of empty blue seats in a stadium (see Figure 16).

Figure 16. One young Visual Explorer participant saw the idea of potential suggested in this image. *Photographs provided by Getty Images, Inc., ©2004. All Rights Reserved.*

For her it was about her commitment to participation: filling the seats and having people want to come to whatever great things were offered in the area. When one of the others in the group saw it, she built on this further (with enthusiastic backing from the others), saying, "Yes, the colour of Dargaville needs to be blue, not red." We came to discover that red is the colour of the gang patches the local gang is currently wearing in town, which are frightening and holding young people (and the district) back. This led to more fascinating conversation about commitment and belonging. This is from a group of young people who hardly know each other and are not accustomed to speaking out at all, let alone in a group of strangers, for an interview.

Our latest use of the images has been with a group of 21- to 28-year-olds in our future leaders programme. We first engaged them in a conversation about moments of vitality and encouraged dialogue to draw out how this may relate to their personal aspirations and hence to the sphere or core of their leadership challenges. After each person had been in the hot seat, they went and literally sat by the fire where there was a coffee table with the postcard-size Visual Explorer images spread out. They each picked a card that represented their aspiration and hopefully where their leadership challenge lay within that. Many of them incorporated the image they chose into a wider strategic picture of their challenge. The exercise was an attempt to represent the complexity of leadership alongside personal passion. The images were an integral aspect of the programme in accomplishing that because some things just cannot be said with the words we have at our disposal—pictures hold those necessary nuances.

Related Applications

- Enabling dialogue
- Facing complex challenges
- Strategic leadership
- Change leadership
- Creative problem solving
- Visioning
- Creating scenarios of the future
- Appreciative inquiry
- Individual coaching
- Team coaching
- Leadership development programs
- Feedback and performance appraisals
- Ethnography and market research
- Retreats and off-site meetings

Additional Resources for This Application

About Learning (Web site).

Amabile. *Growing Up Creative*.

McCarthy. *About Learning*.

Benefits of This Application

- Encourages fun, playful, yet serious dialogue
- Builds direction, alignment, and commitment
- Taps into personal experiences and passions
- Helps frame and illustrate thoughts so they can be shared
- Surfaces individual and group assumptions
- Bridges different contexts and cultures
- Creates new metaphors
- Makes self-disclosure and vulnerability safe
- Produces tangible images that can be reused in paper and digital forms
- Surfaces ideas and new perspectives

There are at least nine reasons to hold an organizational retreat or off-site meeting (Liteman, Campbell, & Liteman, 2006):

1. Explore fundamental concerns
2. Harness the collective creativity of the group
3. Foster change
4. Change perceptions, attitudes, and behavior
5. Correct course when things are going wrong
6. Transform the organization's culture or improve relationships hindering its effectiveness
7. Create a collective vision for the organization
8. Accomplish something that cannot be done by the leader alone
9. Make tough decisions

Visual Explorer works well in addressing these issues in retreat and off-site settings because it enables creative dialogue around difficult subjects, and yet is portable and does not require elaborate setup. Visual Explorer is safe and fun, while drawing people into reflection about fundamental concerns. It also provides a way to preserve the insights that emerge by using the images for documentation and reminders.

Facilitation

The five basic Visual Explorer process steps apply to most of the ways Visual Explorer can be used at a retreat. We recommend keeping the reflection and dialogue elements and not allowing the exercise to become superficial. Depending on the size of the group, several sets of Visual Explorer images may be required (eighty images for every five people is a rough rule of thumb).

The large (letter-size) images work well if there is sufficient space to lay the images flat for browsing on tables and on the floor.

Example of This Application in Action

Merianne Liteman is coauthor, with Sheila Campbell and Jeff Liteman, of *Retreats That Work: Everything You Need to Know about Planning and Leading Great Offsites*. Merianne describes their approach to using Visual Explorer in all kinds of professional and organizational retreats and off-site meetings:

> Because it's so versatile, we find lots of uses for Visual Explorer in retreats. We believe in responding to what's happening in the moment, so sometimes we see uses for Visual Explorer that weren't in our retreat plan. The Visual Explorer deck is almost always in the room with us. I like using the deck to help a group deal with particularly thorny issues about which people might have strong emotions. The introspection that Visual Explorer encourages makes the discussion about these tough issues much richer. Visual Explorer often helps people see all sides of a dilemma rather than be staked in their original positions.
>
> We design a flow into our retreats, peaking in energy as participants make decisions about the issues framed in the retreat. By the end of the retreat, people are tired, but excited about the progress they've made. They're full of good intentions about making a difference when they return to work. But we know they'll also be bombarded by conflicting priorities and an avalanche of interruptions as soon as they get back in the office. We often use Visual Explorer to help them bridge that transition. One of the strong suits of Visual Explorer is that it moves people into a reflective silence in which they can begin to take responsibility for insuring that the decisions made at the retreat take full effect.
>
> When we use Visual Explorer to close a retreat, we display the images on a table at the back of the room during the final break of the day. Participants often wander over to look at the pictures and wonder about their use, but they aren't given any clues upfront. After all the decisions in the retreat have been made, and

- Enabling dialogue
- Facing complex challenges
- Strategic leadership
- Change leadership
- Creative problem solving
- Visioning
- Creating scenarios of the future
- Appreciative inquiry
- Leadership development programs
- Feedback and performance appraisals
- Youth and young adult education

the group has talked about how they'll introduce the results to everyone back at the office, the facilitators talk about how important it will be for each person to keep the retreat spirit alive—and how difficult that can become in the heat of day-to-day work.

Participants are asked to be silent as they write this incomplete sentence at the top of a sheet of paper: "My strongest contributions to keeping the results of this retreat alive will be . . . ." They're given a few moments to think about how to complete it. Before inviting them to choose an image to begin their own reflections, we demonstrate how to use the pictures, usually inviting one of the group to choose an image. This randomness in the choice of image helps reinforce that it doesn't matter what image a person chooses, because, of course, the message evoked is within the person viewing it, not inherent in the picture itself.

After participants have been given time to choose their images and note their reflections, the facilitators can choose from several possible directions. With a small group of fewer than twenty, they can invite every person to share his or her resolutions, which can solidify the respect and closeness that have developed in the retreat. If the work group is likely to encounter serious obstacles in achieving their goals, the facilitators might have them do a second round of reflections based on completing this sentence: "I can foresee some challenges, but I will be able to overcome them by . . . ." These reflections, shared with a small group that works well together, can strengthen the group's resolve to see their decisions through, and help them see how to support each other. In larger groups, we have the participants break into dyads or triads to discuss their Visual Explorer reflections. We feel it's important for people to voice what they're thinking, even if it's not to the whole group. Somehow hearing yourself say it aloud makes the ideas more memorable.

This closing often leads to strong emotions about the retreat. Almost always, some participants are quite moved by the Visual Explorer images. When that happens, we invite people to take the pictures home with them. It wrecks our Visual Explorer decks, but the decks are replaceable; we can stand to lose a few pictures. What we never want to lose is the commitment that the pictures evoke. When we check in with people who have been through a retreat, the students often reference the Visual Explorer images they chose at the end of the program.

Additional Resources for This Application

Liteman, Campbell, & Liteman. "What I See for Me."

Palus & Horth. *Visual Explorer*.

Pasmore & Lafferty. *Developing a Leadership Strategy*.

Selvin et al. "Compendium."

References and Resources

About Learning. The Visual Explorer: Educator's Edition. [Web site]. Retrieved from http://www.aboutlearning.com/teaching-tools/75-the-visual-explorer-educators-edition.html

Ackoff, R. (1978). *The art of problem solving: Accompanied by Ackoff's fables.* New York: John Wiley & Sons.

Amabile, T. M. (1989). *Growing up creative: Nurturing a lifetime of creativity.* New York: Crown.

Appreciative Inquiry Commons (Web site). Retrieved from http://appreciativeinquiry.case.edu/

Argyris, C. (1994). *Knowledge for action.* San Francisco: Jossey-Bass.

Bohm, D. (1990). *On dialogue.* Ojai, CA: David Bohm Seminars.

Brace-Govan, J. (2007). Participant photography in visual ethnography. *International Journal of Market Research, 49*(6), 735–750.

Britton, J. (2010). *Effective group coaching: Tried and tested tools and resources for optimum group coaching results.* Mississauga, Ontario: John Wiley & Sons, Canada.

Bruce Flye. (2010). Retrieved from http://www.positivechange.org/appreciative-inquiry-consultants/bruce-flye.html

Burnside, R. M., & Guthrie, V. A. (1992). *Training for action: A new approach to executive development.* Greensboro, NC: Center for Creative Leadership.

Buron, R. J., & McDonald-Mann, D. (1999). *Giving feedback to subordinates.* Greensboro, NC: Center for Creative Leadership.

Cartwright, T., & Baldwin, D. (2006). *Communicating your vision.* Greensboro, NC: Center for Creative Leadership.

Compendium Institute (Web site). Retrieved from http://compendium.open.ac.uk/institute/community/showcase.htm

Conklin, J. (2006). *Dialogue mapping: Building shared understanding of wicked problems.* West Sussex, UK: John Wiley & Sons.

Cooperrider, D. L., & Whitney, D. (2006). Appreciative inquiry: A positive revolution in change. In P. Holman, T. Devane, & S. Cady (Eds.), *The change handbook: The definitive resource on today's best methods for engaging whole systems* (2nd ed., pp. 73–88). San Francisco: Berrett-Koehler.

Creative Education Foundation (Web site). Retrieved from http://www.creativeeducationfoundation.org/

Criswell, C., & Cartwright, T. (2010). *Creating a vision.* Greensboro, NC: Center for Creative Leadership.

De Ciantis, C. (1995). *Using an art technique to facilitate leadership development.* Greensboro, NC: Center for Creative Leadership.

de Geus, A. (1999). Strategy and learning. *Reflections, 1*(1), 75–81.

De Kluyver, C. A. (2000). *Strategic thinking: An executive perspective.* Upper Saddle River, NJ: Prentice Hall.

Dixon, N. M. (1996). *Perspectives on dialogue: Making talk developmental for individuals and organizations.* Greensboro, NC: Center for Creative Leadership.

Dixon, N. M. (1998). *Dialogue at work: Making talk developmental for people and organizations.* London, UK: Lemos & Crane.

Drath, W. H., McCauley, C., Palus, C. J., Van Velsor, E., O'Connor, P. M. G., & McGuire, J. B. (2008). Direction, alignment, commitment: Toward a more integrative ontology of leadership. *Leadership Quarterly, 19*(6), 635–653.

Drath, W. H., & Palus, C. J. (1994). *Making common sense: Leadership as meaning-making in a community of practice.* Greensboro, NC: Center for Creative Leadership.

Drexler, A., Sibbet, D., & Forrester, R. (2003). *The team performance model.* San Francisco: Grove Consultants International.

Edwards, B. (1987). *Drawing on the artist within: An inspirational and practical guide.* New York: Simon & Schuster.

Ernst, C., & Chrobot-Mason, D. (forthcoming October 2010). *Boundary spanning leadership: Six practices for solving problems, driving innovation, and transforming organizations.* New York: McGraw-Hill Professional.

Ernst, C., & Yip, J. (2009). Boundary spanning leadership: Tactics to bridge social identity groups in organizations. In T. L. Pittinsky (Ed.), *Crossing the divide: Intergroup leadership in a world of difference* (pp. 87–99). Boston, MA: Harvard Business School Press.

Fleenor, J. W., Taylor, S., & Chappelow, C. (2008). *Leveraging the impact of 360-degree feedback.* San Francisco: Pfeiffer.

Geschka, H. (1990). Visual confrontation: Ideas through pictures. In M. Oakley (Ed.), *Design management: A handbook of issues and methods* (pp. 250–254). Oxford: Basil Blackwell.

Global Business Network: Ideas (Web site). Retrieved from http://www.gbn.com/ideas/

Goldsmith, M., & Lyons, L. (Eds.). (2006). *Coaching for leadership: The practice of leadership coaching from the world's greatest coaches* (2nd ed.). San Francisco: Pfeiffer.

Gryskiewicz, S. S. (1999). *Positive turbulence: Developing climates for creativity, innovation, and renewal.* San Francisco: Jossey-Bass.

Gryskiewicz, S., & Taylor, S. (2003). *Making creativity practical: Innovation that gets results.* Greensboro, NC: Center for Creative Leadership.

Hart, E. W., & Miller, K. K. (2001). *Using your executive coach.* Greensboro, NC: Center for Creative Leadership.

Heifetz, R. A. (1994). *Leadership without easy answers.* Cambridge, MA: Harvard University Press.

Hoole, E., & Hannum, K. M. (2008). *Picture this: Using images to gather and communicate evaluation data.* Australasian Evaluation Society (AES) Annual Meeting, 10-12 September 2008, Perth, Australia. Retrieved from http://www.aes.asn.au/conferences/2008/papers/p44.pdf

Hoppe, M. H. (2006). *Active listening: Improve your ability to listen and lead.* Greensboro, NC: Center for Creative Leadership.

Horth, D. M., & Palus, C. J. (2003). Using visuals to build teams. *T+D, 57*(10), 59–63.

Hughes, R. L., & Beatty, K. C. (2005). *Becoming a strategic leader: Your role in your organization's enduring success.* San Francisco: Jossey-Bass.

Hurst, D. K. (1995). *Crisis & renewal: Meeting the challenge of organizational change.* Boston, MA: Harvard Business School Press.

Isaacs, W. (1994). Basic components of a dialogue session. In P. M. Senge, C. Roberts, R. B. Ross, B. J. Smith, & A. Kleiner (Eds.), *The fifth discipline fieldbook: Strategies and tools for building a learning organization* (pp. 377–379). New York: Doubleday.

Isaksen, S. G., Dorval, K. B., & Treffinger, D. J. (1994). *Creative approaches to problem solving.* Dubuque, IA: Kendall/Hunt.

Kahane, A. (2004). *Solving tough problems: An open way of talking, listening, and creating new realities.* San Francisco: Berrett-Koehler.

Kelly, G. A. (1955). *The psychology of personal constructs.* New York: Norton.

Kotter, J. P., & Cohen, D. S. (2002). *The heart of change: Real-life stories of how people change their organizations.* Boston, MA: Harvard Business School Press.

Lakoff, G., & Johnson, M. (1980). *Metaphors we live by.* Chicago: University of Chicago Press.

Liteman, M., Campbell, S., & Liteman, J. (2006). What I see for me. In *Retreats that work: Everything you need to know about planning and leading great offsites* (pp. 410–412). San Francisco: Pfeiffer.

McCarthy, B. (1996). *About learning.* Barrington, IL: Excel, Inc.

McGuire, J. B., & Palus, C. J. (2003). Using dialogue as a tool for better leadership. *Leadership in Action, 23*(1), 8–11.

McGuire, J. B., & Rhodes, G. B. (2009). *Transforming your leadership culture.* San Francisco: Jossey-Bass.

Mieszkowski, K. (1998, February). Wild cards: Report from the futurist. *Fast Company, 13,* 30.

Mintzberg, H. (1987). Crafting strategy. *Harvard Business Review, 65*(4), 66–75.

Morgan, G. (1986). *Images of organizations.* Thousand Oaks, CA: Sage.

Morgan, G. (1997). *Imaginization: New mindsets for seeing, organizing and managing.* Thousand Oaks, CA: Sage.

Morgan, H. J., Harkins, P. J., & Goldsmith, M. (Eds.). (2005). *The art and practice of leadership coaching: 50 top executive coaches reveal their secrets.* Hoboken, NJ: Wiley.

NYU Wagner congratulates the class of 2009, and celebrates convocation at BAM. (2009, May 18). Retrieved from http://wagner.nyu.edu/news/newsStory.php?id=588

Osborn, A. F. (1953). *Applied imagination: Principles and procedures of creative thinking*. New York: Scribner.

Oshry, B. (2007). *Seeing systems: Unlocking the mysteries of organizational life* (2nd ed., Rev.). San Francisco: Berrett-Koehler.

Owen, H. (1997). *Open space technology: A user's guide* (2nd ed.). San Francisco: Berrett-Koehler.

Palus, C. J. (2004). *Artful coaching: An exploration of current one-on-one leader coaching practices.* Proceedings of the Second International Coach Federation Coaching Research Symposium, November 3, 2004, Quebec City, Quebec, Canada.

Palus, C. J. (2006). Artful coaching. In S. Ting & P. Scisco (Eds.), *The CCL handbook of coaching: A guide for the leader coach* (pp. 259–285). San Francisco: Jossey-Bass.

Palus, C. J., & Drath, W. H. (1995). *Evolving leaders: A model for promoting leadership development in programs.* Greensboro, NC: Center for Creative Leadership.

Palus, C. J., & Drath, W. H. (2001). Putting something in the middle: An approach to dialogue. *Reflections, 3*(2), 28–39.

Palus, C. J., & Horth, D. M. (1996). Leading creatively: The art of making sense. *The Journal of Aesthetic Education, 30*(4), 53–68.

Palus, C. J., & Horth, D. M. (2002). *The leader's edge: Six creative competencies for navigating complex challenges.* San Francisco: Jossey-Bass.

Palus, C. J., & Horth, D. M. (2004). Exploration for development. In C. D. McCauley & E. Van Velsor (Eds.), *The Center for Creative Leadership handbook of leadership development* (2nd ed., pp. 438–464). San Francisco: Jossey-Bass.

Palus, C. J., & Horth, D. M. (2005). Leading creatively: The art of making sense. *Ivey Business Journal, 69*(7), 1–8.

Palus, C. J., & Horth, D. M. (2007). Visual explorer. In P. Holman, T. Devane, & S. Cady (Eds.), *The change handbook: The definitive resource on today's best methods for engaging whole systems* (2nd ed., pp. 603–608). San Francisco: Berrett-Koehler.

Palus, C. J., Horth, D. M., Selvin, A. M., & Pulley, M. L. (2003). Exploration for development: Developing leadership by making shared sense of complex challenges. *Consulting Psychology Journal, 55*(1), 26–40.

Parker, M. (1990). *Creating shared vision.* Oslo, Norway: Norwegian Center for Leadership Development.

Parnes, S. J. (Ed.). (1992a). *Source book for creative problem solving: A fifty year digest of proven innovation processes.* Buffalo, NY: Creative Education Foundation.

Parnes, S. J. (1992b). *Visionizing: Innovating your opportunities* (2nd ed.). Buffalo, NY: Creative Education Foundation.

Pasmore, W., & Lafferty, K. (2009). *Developing a leadership strategy: A critical ingredient for organizational success* (White paper). Retrieved from http://www.ccl.org/leadership/pdf/research/LeadershipStrategy.pdf

Pedlar, M., Burgoyne, J., & Boydell, T. (1998). *The learning company: A strategy for sustainable development* (2nd ed.). New York: McGraw-Hill.

Perkins, D. N. (1994). *The intelligent eye: Learning to think by looking at art*. Santa Monica, CA: Getty Center for Education in the Arts.

Peterson, J. L. (1997). *Out of the blue: How to anticipate big future surprises*. Arlington, VA: Danielle LaPorte Book.

Pink, D. H. (1998). Metaphor marketing. *Fast Company, 14*, 214.

Radonsky, T. (2007, November 27). The mystery of the cards. [Web log post]. Retrieved from http://societyofthevav.blogspot.com/2007/11/magic-of-cards.html

Rimanoczy, I., & Turner, E. (2008). *Action reflection learning: Solving real business problems by Connecting learning with earning*. Mountain View, CA: Davies-Black.

Rosinski, P. (2003). *Coaching across cultures: New tools for leveraging national, corporate, and professional differences*. London, UK: Nicholas Brealey.

Schaefer, C. (1993). *Personal identity workshop*. Presented to the Center for Creative Leadership, Greensboro, NC.

Schrage, M. (2000). *Serious play: How the world's best companies simulate to innovate*. Boston, MA: Harvard Business School Press.

Schwartz, D. (1989). Visual ethnography: Using photography in qualitative research. *Qualitative Sociology, 12*(2), 119–154.

Schwartz, P. (1991). *The art of the long view*. New York: Doubleday.

Selvin, A. M. (2008). Performing knowledge art: Understanding collaborative cartography. In A. Okada, S. B. Shum, & T. Sherborne (Eds.), *Knowledge cartography: Software tools and mapping techniques* (pp. 223–248). London, UK: Springer.

Selvin, A. M., & Palus, C. J. (2003, September). Sensemaking techniques in support of leadership development. *InsideKnowledge, 7*(1). Retrieved from http://www.ikmagazine.com

Selvin, A. M., Shum, S. J. B., Horth, D. M., Palus, C. J., & Sierhuis, M. (2002). Knowledge art: Integrating Compendium and Visual Explorer methodologies to explore creative sensemaking. In P. Galle & G. E. Lasker (Eds.), *Knowledge for creative decision-making. Proceedings of a special focus symposium under InterSymp-2002 in Baden-Baden, Germany* (pp. 6–11). Windsor, Ontario: The International Institute for Advanced Studies in Systems Research & Cybernetics.

Selvin, A. M., Shum, S. J. B., Sierhuis, M., Conklin, J., Zimmermann, B., Palus, C. J., Drath, W. H., Horth, D. M., Domingue, J., Motta, E., & Li, G. (2001). Compendium: Making meetings into knowledge events. *Technical Reports*, KM-TR-103. London, UK: The Open University, Knowledge Management Institute.

Sibbet, D. (2010). *Visual meetings: How graphics, sticky notes and idea mapping can transform group productivity*. New York: John Wiley & Sons.

Stavros, J., Cooperrider, D., & Kelley, D. L. (2003, November 1). *Strategic inquiry → Appreciative intent: Inspiration to SOAR: A new framework for strategic planning*. Retrieved from http://appreciativeinquiry.case.edu/practice/executiveDetail.cfm?coid=5331

Suri, J. F., & Howard, S. G. (2006). Going deeper, seeing further: Enhancing ethnographic interpretations to reveal more meaningful opportunities for design. *Journal of Advertising Research, 46*(3), 246–250.

Ting, S., & Scisco, P. (Eds.). *The CCL handbook of coaching: A guide for the leader coach.* San Francisco: Jossey-Bass.

Tornow, W. W., London, M., & the Center for Creative Leadership. (1998). *Maximizing the value of 360-degree feedback: A process for successful individual and organizational development.* San Francisco: Jossey-Bass.

Ullman, M. (1996). *Appreciating dreams: A group approach.* Thousand Oaks, CA: Sage.

van der Heijden, K. (1996). *Scenarios: The art of strategic conversation.* Chichester, England: John Wiley & Sons.

Van Velsor, E., McCauley, C. D., & Ruderman, M. N. (2010). Introduction: Our view of leadership development. In E. Van Velsor, C. D. McCauley, & M. N. Ruderman (Eds.), *The Center for Creative Leadership handbook of leadership development* (3rd ed., pp. 1–26). San Francisco: Jossey-Bass.

Visual Explorer (Resource blog). Retrieved from www.cclexplorer.org

Vogt, E. E., Brown, J., & Isaacs, D. (2003). *The art of powerful questions: Catalyzing insight, innovation, and action.* Mill Valley, CA: Whole Systems Associates. Retrieved from http://www.theworldcafe.com/articles/aopq.pdf

Wack, P. (1985). Scenarios, shooting the rapids. *Harvard Business Review, 63*(6), 139–150.

Weade, R., & Ernst, G. (2001). Pictures of life in classrooms, and the search for metaphors to frame them. *Theory into Practice, 29*(2), 133–140.

Weick, K. E. (1995). *Sensemaking in organizations.* Thousand Oaks, CA: Sage.

Weitzel, S. R. (2000). *Feedback that works: How to build and deliver your message.* Greensboro, NC: Center for Creative Leadership.

What do you see? [Slide show]. (2009, November 1). *New York Times.* Retrieved from http://www.nytimes.com/slideshow/2009/11/01/education/edlife/01Visuals-ss_index.html

Young, D. P., & Dixon, N. M. (1996). *Helping leaders take effective action: A program evaluation.* Greensboro, NC: Center for Creative Leadership.

Zaltman, G. (2003). *How customers think: Essential insights into the mind of the markets.* Boston, MA: Harvard Business School Press.

Zaltman, G., & Coulter, R. H. (1995). Seeing the voice of the customer: Metaphor-based advertising research. *Journal of Advertising Research, 35*(4), 35–51.

Zaltman, G., & Zaltman, L. (2008). *Marketing metaphoria: What deep metaphors reveal about the minds of consumers.* Boston, MA: Harvard Business School Press.

Visual Explorer Worksheet

A. What are your thoughts about how to answer the framing question? What aspects are puzzling or difficult? What has been left out of discussions so far?

B. Selected image number(s): _____. Describe the image: its details, the big picture, what's obvious, what's mysterious, and so on.

C. What's the connection between A and B?

D. Do you have any new insights about the question from your conversations?

Frequently Asked Questions

Q Who can conduct a Visual Explorer session? Will I be able to conduct the Visual Explorer session by myself? What if I lack experience?

A Visual Explorer does not typically require a trained facilitator. It is often self-facilitated by a leader or member of a team, although most sessions benefit from prior experience and skill at facilitation. Visual Explorer is somewhat self-correcting and forgiving, such that the default process tends to be a positive one—a good conversation supported by meaningful imagery. A Visual Explorer facilitator need only support dialogue among the session participants, which usually requires only a beginner's level of facilitation skill.

- -

Q Does Visual Explorer really work?

A Visual Explorer is effective in a wide variety of situations, in part because it's so simple. But its unobtrusiveness and simplicity can be misleading. A dose of skepticism is to be expected and can even prove useful in any process that seeks to question assumptions, as a Visual Explorer session often does. As long as the group's selected topic is relevant and carries a sense of urgency, so that the dialogue is about things that matter most, almost every participant experiences some value from taking part in the Visual Explorer process.

Q What do you tell participants when setting up the exercise?

A You need to address the two main questions the group will have

- Why are we doing this activity?
- What are the instructions?

Just give a brief, clear rationale based on addressing some shared issue, with Visual Explorer as merely one tool for looking at the issue. Don't position Visual Explorer as some kind of magic bullet. The instruction you give can vary according to the group and the specific application, but you can quickly go over the process at the beginning of the session.

Q What do you tell people who are skeptical of the value of Visual Explorer?

A We actually invite people to be skeptical, but we also invite them to hold their skepticism lightly and enter the experience "as if it made sense." One time a scientist we worked with voiced his skepticism, which we welcomed and responded to, and he replied, "Not proven. But carry on!"

Q Is Visual Explorer a game, or is it a simulation?

A Visual Explorer is not in itself a team exercise, game, or simulation. There is no single right way to use it. It's a flexible tool used to facilitate a good conversation.

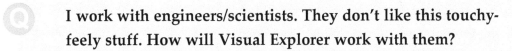

Q **I work with engineers/scientists. They don't like this touchy-feely stuff. How will Visual Explorer work with them?**

A Scientists who have used Visual Explorer often recognize its combined effect of image, intuition, and metaphor as related to scientific creativity. The depth of dialogue achieved in Visual Explorer sessions convinces people from all kinds of disciplines of its value. Chuck Palus and David Horth are scientists and engineers by background. They often find that once the engineers and scientists have got past the skepticism phase (in which their skepticism has been invited), they rapidly dive deeper into conversations. One conversation stimulated by Visual Explorer was supposed to last no more than ninety minutes but went on with everyone deeply engaged for eight hours.

- -

Q **I work with executives. They don't like this touchy-feely stuff. How will Visual Explorer work with them?**

A Because Visual Explorer is not an exercise but adapts to the purposes at hand, it takes on a serious feel when used in these kinds of situations. Executives don't like being distracted from work, but as they experience the way in which Visual Explorer helps them grasp challenges and create new options, they become convinced of its value. One experienced Visual Explorer facilitator has described how he plays with a deck of Visual Explorer images without revealing what it is when working with executives and they become intrigued and ask what he's playing with. After a quick demonstration, these senior leaders eagerly embrace it.

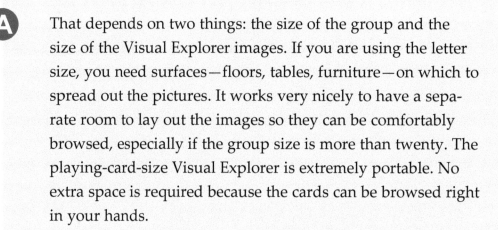

Q How much space does it require?

A That depends on two things: the size of the group and the size of the Visual Explorer images. If you are using the letter size, you need surfaces—floors, tables, furniture—on which to spread out the pictures. It works very nicely to have a separate room to lay out the images so they can be comfortably browsed, especially if the group size is more than twenty. The playing-card-size Visual Explorer is extremely portable. No extra space is required because the cards can be browsed right in your hands.

- -

Q How much advance planning does a Visual Explorer session require?

A Those who know Visual Explorer reasonably well can have it as a tool "in their back pocket" with no advance planning whatsoever. More typically, the planning time depends on whether it has been specifically designed into a training program or organizational intervention.

- -

Q How much time is needed to conduct a Visual Explorer session?

A The session itself can be done in as little as an hour; anticipate a good conversation and allow at least ninety minutes. Groups often extend the dialogue productively for hours and hours.

Can I run a session faster than that?

Do not shortcut the sharing of images during the Visual Explorer session if dialogue is the goal. Paying careful attention to the images is important for getting past the surface and engaging with each other in a way that supports dialogue. It takes time to reach that stage of conversation.

About the Authors

Charles J. Palus is a senior enterprise associate at the Center for Creative Leadership. He conducts research on interdependent leadership and creates innovations for CCL's organization leadership development practice. He is the coauthor of *The Leader's Edge: Six Creative Competencies for Navigating Complex Challenges*. He received his B.S. in chemical engineering from the Pennsylvania State University and his Ph.D. in adult developmental psychology from Boston College.

David Magellan Horth is a senior enterprise associate at the Center for Creative Leadership. He is a program designer and an accomplished trainer in a range of custom and open-enrollment programs. He is the coauthor of *The Leader's Edge: Six Creative Competencies for Navigating Complex Challenges*. He holds a B.Sc. (Hons) from the University of Surrey in England.

CPSIA information can be obtained
at www.ICGtesting.com
Printed in the USA
BVHW020513040720
582948BV00004BA/219